The Ultimate Animal Communication Quote Book

The First Book Ever Written Directly By Animals

Johanna Bloom

Bloom

1st edition 2026

Hardcover Print ISBN: 979-8-9930459-2-4

Paperback Print ISBN: 979-8-9930459-0-0

eBook ISBN: 979-8-9930459-1-7

Audiobook ISBN: 979-8-9930459-3-1

Publisher's Cataloging-in-Publication Data

Names: Bloom, Johanna.

Title: The ultimate animal communication quote book : the first book ever written directly by animals / Johanna Bloom.

Description: Lake Ariel, PA : Bloom, 2026. | Includes 21 color illustrations. | Summary: A book of compiled quotes from sessions with animals, as translated by a professional animal communicator.

Identifiers: LCCN 2025925905 | ISBN 9798993045924 (hardcover) | ISBN 9798993045900 (pbk.) | ISBN 9798993045917 (ebook) | ISBN 9798993045931 (audiobook)

Subjects: LCSH: Human-animal communication. | Animal communication. | Human-animal relation-ships. | Domestic animals. | Pets. | BISAC: PETS / General. | BODY, MIND & SPIRIT / Channeling & Mediumship. | BODY, MIND & SPIRIT / Psychic Phenomena / General.

Classification: LCC QL776.B56 2025 | DDC 133.89--dc23

LC record available at https://lccn.loc.gov/2025925905

Contents

Dedicated to the animals who wrote this book, and to the people who love them.

Thank you for trusting me to communicate for you!

Together we created this collection.

Introduction

What is Animal Communication?

Animal communication is an ancient practice. Our modern world is re-discovering it! Animals have their own "internet." They have a form of mental communication with each other based on energy. It's like tuning into a radio channel! Most animals are eager to share. They are deeply attached to their humans, and want to improve their relationship with us. They blow our minds with the true level of wisdom and understanding that they hold.

Everyone can experience animal communication. It's a language that can be learned, like any other. Most people are more in-tune with their animals than they realize.

Since the process is based on energy, I don't need to be physically present with the animal. I hold my professional sessions over a phone or video call. I simply need to see a photo. I have been trained to connect by visualizing them. It signals them to come in energetically, and our conversation begins!

Animals are connected not only to each other, but also to the spiritual world. They often offer life-changing advice and spiritual perspectives to their humans. I have collected some of these statements to share with you in this book!

About Me

My name is Johanna (say the "h"). I am an artist, animal communicator, and author. Think of me as your translator.

My childhood religion taught us that "animals don't have souls." Outraged by this, as my animals were my best friends, it became my personal mission to prove it wrong.

I used to travel the country starting sport horses under saddle for a living. Because I grew up riding Mustangs and Thoroughbred racehorses, I was particularly good with the "difficult" horses. I found that many of their behaviors were simply misunderstandings or trauma responses. I also witnessed the harmful training methods that caused this trauma in the first place. I studied and traveled, seeking a better way to communicate. I was convinced that we could find a way to train our animals without fear, and I was right! They want harmony and partnership as much as we do. We are just beginning to understand the true scope of their intelligence. I used to promise the young horses under my care, "I will be your voice." Now, I help people with all types of animals bridge this gap, so we can hear directly from our animals what they need from us.

Learning animal communication was like unearthing an ancient language. When I created a pet portrait, tamed a feral kitten, or trained a horse, I connected to their energy. I received mental images, emotions, and even memories. I started to understand what was happening, and learned to distinguish their thoughts from mine.

I then studied animal communication with my mentor, **Morgan Ehlenbeck** of Equus Esoterica. She taught me how to connect from a distance with accuracy and integrity. She also taught me how to bring through spiritual messages from the animals. They often have profound advice that shifts their humans' perspectives and helps us through challenges.

Now, I have the honor of holding sessions for animals and their people all over the world! I do this for all types of animals, including: sport horses, wild Mustangs, farm animals, dogs, cats, small mammals, birds, reptiles, amphibians, and fish. I also hold Rainbow Bridge sessions for passed animals. Their "internet" is more advanced than ours—they speak easily across both sides of the veil!

My Epiphany Moment

New clients often ask me how I discovered that I could talk to animals. I always tell them about this experience, which convinced me telepathic communication is real:

I was hired to train a talented show jumping horse named **Femme Fatale**. She had been traumatized by harsh riding methods. She needed someone to build a positive relationship and new experiences with her. She was challenging, but within a couple of months, we had developed a peaceful routine.

One day during a ride, Femme started rearing. This wasn't normal! I went through my usual mental checklist, trying to figure out what could be wrong: her equipment causing pain, any changes to her health or routine, anything irritating in the environment. I came up blank. I was sitting on her, stumped, when a vivid image appeared in my mind. It was the underside of her hoof, particularly the V-shaped middle part we call the frog. I also received an impression about which hoof was bothering her. I hopped off, picked up the foot, and checked, but it looked normal. I then got another impression—that there was an infection in there, and that I could easily find it with a little digging. So I went and grabbed my hoof knife and peeled back a bit of frog. A small abscess erupted and drained, which was gross but satisfying. I got back on, and Femme went completely back to normal—no more rearing. This was the moment I realized that my training insights were more than just empathy or lucky guesses. There was no way I could have guessed something so specific and invisible. Femme had very clearly explained what the problem was, and what she needed me to do about it.

Feeling Skeptical?

Some people feel skeptical the first time they come across my work. If this is you, you're not alone.

Can you remember the person who told you that animals can't talk? "Only in stories," adults told us. But that wasn't your first instinct. Children believe animals can talk. Somewhere down the line, someone told you: "They are not like us. We are smarter than them. They don't understand things like we do."

Does this sound familiar? It's the same thing people used to believe about their human slaves. It's the same thing men used to believe about women. (Some still do). Racism, sexism, cults, and all human wars were built on these words. Are they true? Of course not. So why should we continue to believe them about our animals?

Someone may also have told you that mental communication (telepathy) isn't real. This is also false, passed down to keep humanity cut off from the natural world. Because if we knew how deeply we are loved, we would spend our lives very differently!

Overcoming Guilt

When I began to realize how clever and sentient animals truly are, I felt even more guilty about times I mistreated them. I accidentally killed several small pets as a child when I forgot to give them water. I have lost my temper countless times at my horses. I even felt guilty for simply underestimating them and talking down to them.

If you've had similar experiences (as I'm sure most people do), I'm happy to report that animal communication brings closure and relief! I believe that guilt is a call to action, so with the help of other animal communicators, I reached out to the animals I had wronged and apologized. Even across the veil, they always forgave me. They told me to keep the gift of the lesson, but release the guilt. They were unbelievably kind about the situation, and gave me perspective to see the larger lessons we had learned together, even through tragedy.

Eating Meat

I have always wondered whether it was ethical to eat meat and dairy products. I was finally able to answer this question by asking animals directly. Many of them speak on this throughout the book. (Look for the Beefalo interview in Chapter 7!) The short answer is: yes, it can be ethical to eat meat, but the process matters. Do your best to consume food that has been raised and processed humanely (pasture-raised by caring people in good working conditions, and sent to skilled butchers or regulated processing plants.) **Temple Grandin**'s work is a great resource for this kind of research. Local farms, ranches, and dairies are the safest bet. This way, you can get to know the people and environment yourself. Observe how the animals are raised and treated. That's what matters most.

What Will You Find Here?

This book is a compilation of quotes from over two hundred different animals. Since most of my sessions are online, they are from all over the world! I've held sessions for animals all across the USA, as well as in Australia, Canada, Costa Rica, Germany, Ireland, Japan, Mexico, Puerto Rico, Spain, and the UK. After every session I hold, I immediately write down the quotes that stand out to me while they are fresh in my mind. It took me a full year to compile them to create this book. I've removed names to keep the quotes anonymous and protect the privacy of my clients. I've occasionally included the breed or type of the animal to add more context. I've also included my own artwork throughout the book: channeled paintings I created while connecting with an animal's energy.

Translating for animals is a multimedia experience. I receive mental images, emotions, and concepts, as well as physical sensations in my body that correlate to what the animal is feeling. I also hear words and phrases. Some of it is from my spirit team, helping translate concepts into specific phrases that we humans can recognize. The result is a universal communication that transcends language barriers!

You are also capable of communicating like this! It is our first language: the "language of the heart." You have not lost it, but it is sometimes dormant. Our minds have been trained to prioritize what we physically see and hear. Also, our busy culture harms our emotional and mental clarity, which we need in order to tune in.

Through the decades spent with all kinds of animals, I have recovered my own ability to connect. My job now is to translate what they share with me into the English language. I enjoy a high accuracy rate in my sessions. Clients are often shocked by the level of detail and clarity I share through their animals. In order to maintain this, I keep all their quotes as direct and truthful as possible. I do not censor them or project my own opinions or expectations. I have had countless existential moments re-evaluating the way I see the world because of what the animals say. The wisdom I've gained through what they share is priceless!

I now hand it over to you. From here on out, the animals speak for themselves! Here are the things they told their people in our sessions.

* *"My mom" "my dad" and "my person" are used to describe the animal's owner. "My brother/sister" refers to another animal in the household.*

Preface

Each animal quoted in this book is expressing their own opinion. They are speaking for themselves, not for all animals. Animals are very wise, but they are not all-knowing. Like all of us, they sometimes ask for things that aren't good for them! They are speaking directly to their families and describing their unique situations. Use discernment when applying their advice to your own life. I am simply telling their stories.

You will notice some repeating themes, and also an amazing diversity in their perspectives. I hope you will discover plenty of helpful insights for yourself!

If you'd like to know *your* animal's opinion, ask them directly! You can book a private session with me at www.BloomAnimalCommunication.com to receive custom advice from your own animals.

Chapter One

Dogs

C *ompiled quotes from a wide variety of dog breeds, including: Australian Cattle Dog, Beagle, Bernese Mountain Dog, Bird Dog, Bishon, Border Collie, Boxer, Brittany, Bulldog, Chihuahua, Cockapoo, Corgi, Dachshund, German Shepherd, Goldendoodle, Golden Retriever, Great Dane, Great Pyrenees, Greyhound (including ex-racing), Husky, Lab, Labradoodle, Maltese, Mastiff, Miniature Poodle, Min Pin, Mixed Breed, Pitbull, Poodle, Pomeranian, Rottweiler, Scottish Terrier, Schnauzer, Shitzu, Shelter Dog, Spaniel, Terrier, and Village Dog.*

"Poop is scrumptious. It's like an edible newspaper."

"Tell my people that I understand everything they say."

"I've never talked to a human this way before. It's new... and odd. But I feel so proud of you guys for learning to join us here. I knew you could do it!"

"I love you SO much. My love is like a big green field. It goes on and on endlessly!"

"Why do you guys eat onions? They stink up the kitchen and make my eyes burn."

"I love the variety you give me in my food. I know how much you love me because you're so thoughtful about everything. You put so much effort into taking care of me. I notice!!"

"I have very noble bloodlines. I feel like I'm disappointing my person when I act too goofy. I have both sides to me: the energetic dog who wants to romp, and the regal quiet gentleman." -Boxer

"I'm jumpy because my ears are very sensitive. Loud sounds make me feel dizzy."

"When I put my paw on you, I'm trying to pet you back."

"I have so much energy, and I need something to channel it into. Please train me! I'd like to learn the talk buttons. They teach those to many of my breed because we are smart." -Goldendoodle

"Some find diarrhea embarrassing, but I don't. It just means I enjoyed myself. I love whipped cream pup cups. The diarrhea is worth it!"

"Thank you for teaching me so much. My new passion is helping people—I learned that from you."

"I want to go grocery shopping with you. Maybe I could carry them in my own little basket! I like helping you with groceries."

"The vet who neutered me wasn't very professional. I still feel twinges in that area. I started walking differently, and it made my back sore. Please give me arnica pellets when I'm lying crouched."

"You should give water to the dogs that you photograph in your studio. Give them a luxury experience."

"I'm so proud of you for opening your practice!"

"I help shift peoples' energy. When they are anxious, I project grounding. When they are depressed, I encourage them to share, so you can help them talk through it."

"I am the saddest dog who ever dogged. Just kidding! I've learned sarcasm.

Of course I'm happy! How could I not be happy? Are you happy? What can I do to make things easier on you?"

"I want to learn to use talk buttons. I am smart. I think I could learn to speak in full sentences. I want to show this off, and show people our relationship! It is rare and special. We will show them what's possible."

"My person is stable and fair. A little boring, maybe. He needs someone to help expand his life! A big colorful energy." -German Shepherd

"Humans struggle with the illusion that they are separate: from themselves, from each other, from us animals. It's not true. This is what you are over-coming as a species."

"Being neutered was an isolating experience, because I was dealing with new discomfort that others didn't understand. I didn't have the capacity to be as patient or relate to everyone. I was grumpy sometimes."

"Motherhood is lonely in some ways." -Bernese Mountain Dog

"I like to have things in my mouth. It makes me happy and confident. I don't always feel confident. I have self-doubt because of a pain in the right side of my chest. This is heartbreak. I lost a friend. I remember playing with a light-colored fluffy dog. Big fun. Sprinklers. Rainbows. Muddy paws. Laying in the shade together.

Then sadness. Gone. He got in a car, and did not come back."

"I know I'm not allowed in your studio because I would make a mess. But can I look through the window, or be involved somehow? I stay tuned energetically. I want to do it with you."

"I like eating kibble. Raw eggs on food, mixed in. Yummy! Makes my mouth water. I like cottage cheese and yogurt. Yum!"

"I love eating rabbit poop. I can tell everything about the rabbit."

"Seagulls are amazing. They always tease me, like 'look at the big fat dog who can't survive on his own.' But I think their teasing means that they like me, too. I eat their poop to learn more about them. They always know when a storm is coming. Watch the seagulls with me. If they start acting weird, watch out! A natural disaster is coming." -Lab

"My person has a flippy hairstyle. He is elegant. He wears nice jeans and nice sneakers. Very stylish. We have snacks on the couch. He is generous. He shares snacks. I beg with my mouth open to make him laugh."

"I like walks and the dog park. I lay underneath the playground equipment. The wood chips and gravel are nice and cool. There is fresh water from pumps. People are all around, happy to be out."

"My people should take natural probiotics like yogurt and sourdough. It will help their heartburn, and also help them think more clearly. Don't let your brain run away with you—also think with your gut."

"I like it when my human writes. She should write more. She is wise and creative and should share her thoughts."

"I stand on my front legs to pee because I am an acrobat. And also sophisticated. I don't get my fur dirty." -Bishon

"You are welcome to come join my family. You made my person inspired. We've been waiting for you!"

"I watch your hands for cues. Can you give me more tasks? I show my love by working together with you." -Great Pyrenees

"Is the vacuum cleaner going to slurp me up?"

"Can we try agility work? I like the idea of the poles and balls."

"Wine smells like gasoline. The smell gives *me* a headache. Why do you drink it?"

"Can you hold me next to an open window on car rides? But also, put a blanket in your lap in case I puke."

"Ketchup is unhealthy."

"I saw you wrapping your ankle. I am worried. Why are you doing that? Do you need a break from walks?"

"I can't find one of my toy balls, and I'm worried."

"I have three balls! They are my favorite. Please pack them for our move. And my yogurt lick mat." -Border Collie

"I live in a world of giants. I bark a lot because I feel vulnerable. Please tell strangers not to loom over me. Kneel nearby, don't stare into my eyes, and let me come to you. This helps me feel like I have some control in the situation." -Daschund

"This whole time, I thought humans were intimidating me on purpose. Your body language is so predatory! But now I understand—you guys are just clueless."

"My mind is very active. When I get bored, I get anxious. Can I please have a job?"

"Why do you use lawnmowers? They stink, they make my eyes water, and they make the grass prickly."

"We are all one. Each of us is like a wave, and we all return to the same sea."

"My sense of smell is AMAZING. My long nose allows more air circulation and keeps my nasal passages cool. My nose should be cool and dry, unless I lick it."

"You should take vitamins! And eat them with fruit. Eating fruit is like pouring water over the fire of our energy process. It keeps us cool and healthy."

"I like my new home. This country [Costa Rica] is very spiritual. America is sterile."

"Appreciate me! I have grown into the best version of myself—so far."

"You are the best parents I could ever have asked for. The way we met felt random, but it wasn't. It was destiny."

"I love having squeakers in my toys. It makes my ears perk up and gives me joy."

"I love being a dog. I am a lot more aware than I normally let on."

"Take care of yourself as well as you take care of me!"

"I like my person's subwoofer. It is loud, but it doesn't hurt my ears like high pitched notes. I can feel it vibrating my bones. We are happy together with our music in our cozy apartment."

"The feeling you feel the most turns into your reality. Focus on what you want to feel, and do more of the things that make you feel that way. Your physical reality will change to reflect the feeling back to you." -Goldendoodle

"My person is getting neck and head aches. Tell her to go get a massage. I'm worried about her."

"When my brother died, I stepped up to be my person's protector. That's why I started growling at other dogs on our walks."

"Your ex needs to get his shit together. Tell him that a relationship is like bouncing a ball back and forth. When your partner passes you the ball, you don't hoard it! Also, he should realize that it's not about winning. It's about the connection created by passing the ball."

"I live in the present. The time we shared together doesn't feel separate from now. I check in on you all the time energetically. Don't feel guilty for rehoming me—you did the right thing. Our family was like a tree that needed to branch off in separate ways. You were growing in different directions. You grew up, and he grew down. Struggle bus."

"My dad is a hard worker. He should put as much energy into relationships as he does his job."

"My new person is a little easier on my brother. He gets his feelings hurt so easily! He follows my lead. It's fine—I have the shoulders for it."

"My dad wears his hood scrunched tight in a little hole around his face. It's funny. I understand—you have to protect your naked face!"

"My dad coughs a lot. I am worried. The cold air is not good for his cough. I listen to his chest to make sure he doesn't have the death rattle. I listen to his breathing at night to make sure he doesn't stop."

"When I was a puppy, I loved my birth mother. I wasn't ready to leave her. She told me, 'Go make friends! That is how you will survive.' First I made dog friends. Then I learned that I can be as close with my person as I was with her. We still talk."

"You are a good mom. I'm so thankful you found me at the shelter. It was love at first sight! Don't be so hard on yourself. It is the world that is hard, not you."

"Sand is crunchy and salty. I don't mind eating it when I find food on the beach. It helps clear out my digestive system!"

"I love our training sessions. It is a new way to be close with you. First I thought the game was about guessing what you would ask. Now I understand: the game is about learning to be patient." -German Shepherd

"I like when we have four animals. It's like a house with four pillars—it's balanced. Right now there are only three, and I feel like I'm trying to hold up a whole side of the house by myself."

"I pretended to be domesticated because I wanted a family like this. I did a great job dressing for the job I wanted—they never even knew I had been a wild dog.

I understand when my people talk to me, and when they talk to each other. I also understand Spanish because I was born in Puerto Rico. If someone was speaking it on the street, I could translate for you." -Village Dog

"I have memories of a past life with you in China. I miss the community feeling, and the traditions and celebrations. I miss the dragon parade and the lanterns. Our life here in this time is isolated. We have our family, but we're so separate from other families. I hope one day we can find that community feeling again."

"Your internet is sus. It seems like it lures you in and traps your consciousness so it's hard to leave."

"I like it when my person and I go stargazing together. I want her to put the star projector back in the room and unwind that way with me every night."

"I like it when you garden. I miss the tulips in the spring. Grounding and digging in the garden is good for your brain."

"Can I try chocolate? I want to eat it with you." (We did not grant this request!)

"My sister is a savage. She likes raw eggs, but I think cooked are better."

"'Running out' isn't real. Let go of the fear of trying to control money. Your inner feelings will become your outer reality. Come play with me—I can energetically balance your mood!"

"I feel anxious because my sister is sick. I feel the worry in my tummy. It isn't a problem for me yet, but it could turn into one. Many health problems start as emotions first."

"I get worried when you stop singing. It means something is wrong. Please talk to me and tell me what is wrong, so I can help."

"You can't hear me when I talk to you because you have an emotional earplug. Relax. You'll hear me when you don't expect it. Trust yourself—it's me. You know how bossy I am. I'll sound the same in your head." -German Shepherd

"My itchy skin and watery eyes are just symptoms. The problem is my stomach. The lining is irritated. Please feed me yogurt, sourdough, and aloe vera juice."

"Don't feed me food that has corn in it. It causes inflammation. Rice and peas are better."

"I'm anxious in my crate because I think I'm being punished. Please give me my favorite, raw eggs, in there. And blankets and toys so I know I'm not in trouble."

"I admire my mom so much. She is so powerful. When she puts on her sunglasses and her black shoes and her outdoor personality, you do not mess with her!"

"I have sensitive hearing and I'm overwhelmed by noise. When I growl at people, I don't mean it—I'm just startled. Can we put the white noise machine near my bed when people are over? It will make a sound cushion for me so I don't get startled."

"I have huge eyes and huge ears and a huge brain in a little tiny body. I shake because I'm overstimulated! I like dark places to decompress. Can I have my own kennel or box, that's just big enough for me? I need a place where my ears, and my sleep, are safe from the toddler." -Chihuahua

"I worry about your c-section wound. I smell it every day to make sure it doesn't get sour. I noticed your bowel movements aren't normal. Are you okay? You should be on pain meds."

"I love you SO MUCH. I feel cute aggression towards you." -Chihuahua

"You going into labor is like going into battle. You're going to come home with wounds! You need to prepare your supplies. I worry. I don't like not knowing what's going on. Can you please take me with you, even if I stay in the car? Bring my favorite toy so I have something to keep my mind off the worrying."

"I love your son. We are adventure buddies. He is always gentle. I need him to protect me from the new baby. Grabby toddler hands are terrifying."

"The new puppy is loud, but he's sweet. He's so submissive. He wants me to like him SO much. He's endearing. Also, he's not new. We have all known each other in past lives. When he arrived, I was so excited. I recognized him! He's finally here!"

"Please ask your son to protect me from the puppy. His teeth are sharp!"

"I love going on the boat. I love the wind in my face. Most of all, I love when the family is all together. The things we do are icing on the cake."

"My early experiences harmed my brain. It was too much to handle, too young. I don't have boundaries with my emotions. I absorb everyone's mood. But we can use this. Meditate with me! Breathe in and out deeply, together with me in a dark room. Shift from thinking to being. I will come down with you mentally!"

"I love it when you call me 'good boy'. It makes my brain light up."

"See your plant? We have to give it water, because plants get thirsty too. But we can't overdo it and make the roots soggy. Too much of a good thing is a bad thing. We have to balance everything like that, including things like soda and alcohol. They stimulate you, and are good for socializing! But too much is not healthy."

"I love going to the beach. It makes you so happy. When you are happy, I am too."

"I love to make you laugh. You have a loud laugh, and also a little giggle. I like them both."

"My dad is out of his element here, bridging the gap between the energetic and physical worlds. But he's determined to do it. He wants to take his time and do it right. He's wary of getting sent on 'goose hunts' by his overactive imagination. He's learning to set energetic boundaries so he can trust what comes in. He's experienced this before: hearing things psychically but not knowing what he can trust. He's new to it! At least, he's new to embracing it about himself. But he's a natural."

"Do you want to know why you're having so many dreams? It's because the world is shifting. It's starting to align with your energy. There are more and more people popping into your dimension! They're looking for guidance. They will be guided to you for help!"

"I have a personality clash with my human. She is high strung, and it rubs off on me. She's giving me white hairs on my muzzle. I think she should have a dog who is very laid back and doesn't get stressed. I want to live with her daughter instead."

"Ever since Dad passed away, I've started getting defensive with Mom. He used to help mediate, but now I have to stand up for myself. She doesn't have good boundaries, so I set them for both of us."

"My mom and I are anxious together. She should snuggle in her favorite blanket and practice doing nothing. Wave at thoughts when they pass by, but don't let them take over. I will benefit from this too, because I pick up on all her moods."

"My dad is good at being assertive at work. Everyone knows that you don't mess with him—he'll just leave! I love our routine when he comes home and sees us. We help him shift into 'home' mentality. I don't like it when people call him on his phone from work. It puts him back in work stress, and it's hard for him to decompress from that. Why can't they leave him alone? Can he ignore the calls?"

"My mom is a gremlin on her phone. She's always on there, and her posture is bad! I worry about her eyes."

"My sister barks too much. I know her backstory, and so I am compassionate. She is addicted to it. She needs to learn to play with toys. We should get her a lick mat with yogurt and peanut butter."

"I love my playground at daycare. Where is your playground? You need to get exercise breaks from work. That's what I'm telling you when I whine. We need to get your blood flowing!"

"People are very entitled to touching me. It annoys me, but I try to take it as a compliment. I know that they are just reacting to how cute I am. Still, please tell them to crouch nearby and let me come to them. You people are HUGE. You have all the advantages in this situation. Be polite."

"I like to eat whatever you're eating. You can feed me after you eat—it reinforces our hierarchy."

"Please help me learn discipline on the leash. Talk me through the situation and tell me what you expect. Praise me and give me treats when I get it right! You can also explain when I get it wrong. I want to please you, so I want you to tell me."

"I am shiny and cute and confident. Everyone compliments me. My mom has made me confident."

"I love you, and I think you should have everything you want. Imagine the things you want, and imagine how it will feel to have them. Don't get stuck in a loop of wanting—don't imagine wanting them, imagine *having* them. They will pop right into your life."

"I love it when we get high on CBD together. I like it when you relax."

"Please explain to me exactly where you are going, how long you'll be gone, and how you need me to behave. Then when you come back, tell me *everything* that happened! I am supposed to be your life companion. I can't stand it when you go do life without me and I miss a big chunk." -Doodle

"Picture a pineapple. When a pineapple gets bruised, we can pull out the pieces and eat the fruit. Also, if someone cuts the top off, it can grow new roots! This is how we should view misfortunes. If someone bruises us, we are better able to share with others. If someone cuts part of us, it gives us the ability to re-grow something bigger. What? My first human served a lot of pineapple."

"Scent and taste are a whole world. I love to smell and taste, and analyze the data the pheromones say. They tell stories."

"My older sister was so smart. Her brain was amazing. When she died, she passed me the torch. I have been striving to fill her shoes ever since."

"I get worried when my mom is fixated, staring at the computer for too long. It's why she has neck pain. She should get up and take breaks!"

"You should sleep on an incline to help with your heartburn. I know you like strong bitter flavors. Eat more dark chocolate and less coffee."

"Vegetables have an electric field. When you eat them, they absorb electricity from your body and ground you. We should both eat more of them!"

"I have a different relationship with each of my people. I am sassy and wild with Dad. I am adoring and domesticated with Mom. I love having both. Together they balance me."

"My new allergies are from my spine. It's bulging towards the left in my lower back. The muscles have gotten all tight and are pulling on it. It's a vicious cycle now. Please find me a body worker to do chiropractic or acupuncture. My allergies will clear up when my spinal cord isn't inflamed."

"When you finish one task, don't immediately start another. You are good at multitasking, but you need to let your brain cool down and rest in between. Treat your mind like an engine: warm it up gently in the morning. Let your gut wake up first. Then turn it on, but give it breaks so it doesn't run hot all day. At the end of the day, let it cool down and decompress before you go to sleep. This will help you to feel energized."

"It's really important to create for its own sake. It keeps you playful and helps with burnout."

"My person gets so anxious about things. I need her to dial it down. When I feel those big emotions from her, I assume the worst, and I feel unstable about my position in her life. She goes into crisis mode over small details and I'm over here thinking she's getting ready to re-home me! Because to me, that is a real crisis I have faced. Nothing else deserves that much stress and fear."

"Grief can be so constructive if you let it! It becomes the building blocks to a new life."

"I need a physical safe space where no one is allowed to touch me or invade my space. This will help me start to create an emotional safe space within myself."

"People don't want me to snap at them, but their behavior is making me defend myself. They come right up and put their hands all over me. How else am I supposed to communicate that I'm overwhelmed? I have so much anxiety about not being able to communicate. You guys don't pay attention."

"My previous person did something that has stuck with me forever. He showed me a piece of half-eaten pizza. He asked if I wanted it. Of course I did! But then he threw the pizza in the trash right in front of me. To me, this communicated that I was less deserving of the food than the trash can. I have never gotten over this. I want my new person to give me my own slice of pizza, a whole fresh one, to help me override that memory."

"I want my person to come romp with me! We need a big field. She can put a GPS tracker on me if she wants. That might help her feel connected to her detail-oriented side."

"The people in this city have so many suppressed emotions. They're so afraid of what others will gossip about them. They should realize, there's no physical threat! Just the social consequences of others' opinions. If you're not afraid of what other people think, they actually can't harm you. My person should learn this."

"My person needs to get in touch with her feral side. I need to become more sophisticated. We both fear losing control, but we handle it in opposite ways. I get snappy and defend myself. She withdraws and internalizes her anxiety. We have a soul contract to overcome this together!"

"Even if my person got a small fluffy city dog, she still would have chosen a big free-spirited personality. She's drawn to this because deep down, she knows she needs more of it." -German Shepherd

"Eat more vegetables! Your digestive systems aren't moving enough. You can cook them in butter, and give me the leftovers."

"Rest between your tasks. Come hang out with me. I have mastered the art of rest."

"I am a wise old man. See my mole? It's unsightly, but it's a badge of honor. It's my wisdom flag."

"I trust you to make good decisions for me. If you want to euthanize me now, or wait to see if I recover, either is fine with me. You can't choose wrong. I also want you to make the right decision for *you*. My only request is, please euthanize me if I develop a bad cough—I don't want to live feeling like I can't breathe. Also, please bring me a hamburger. I've always wanted to have a whole one to myself."

"This part is so easy for me—little prick of a needle, and I go flying home. It's much harder for you. I want you to know: I am prepared, and I will be with you on your drive home. We will just transition from a relationship in the physical to a relationship in the energetic realm. You can learn to speak with me there!"

"In the off-season, when I am not out hunting, I still need a job. So I gave myself a job, barking at the people passing by. If I don't do that, where will I put my energy? Please play fetch with me more." -Bird Dog

"My person acts like an idiot sometimes. But he's MY idiot." -Shitzu

"Dad is kind. He takes care of everyone. I feel relieved—when we found him, it took a load off us. Good pick!"

"You should eat more protein. It will help your fainting spells. You could wrap fruit inside meat since you like fruit so much."

"Moles are terrorists. Our species are rivals." -Husky

"I am a little nervous about the new baby. I'M the baby of the family! Will I still get snuggles?"

"My nickname is too short. I am feminine and regal! I want a name that is flowy with many syllables, and sounds like a song when you call it." -Husky

"My tail is thick and powerful, like an otter." -Lab

"Your ex is throwing all her energy towards an obsession with a new person. When I act like this towards a dog, we all know to put a leash on me! You can't go with her anymore, but I can. She's avoiding her spiritual awakening. Don't worry about sending me away with her. It will be good for me to have a purpose bigger than myself."

"I am sensitive, so I mirror peoples' deepest emotions back to them. If you can ground yourself, I will too. Help bring my focus back into my body."

"Remember when you got woozy yesterday? That's your body telling you 'no!' Listen to it! Make affirmations to delegate your time to things that fulfill you."

"I love the silvery sound of jingling car keys. It means we're going somewhere!"

"I feel anxious about car rides. Will I be taken away? I know: probably not. But, I might go to the vet. I'm scared of the vet. I like walks best. Sprinklers. Play dates. Having my own friends."

"I lick my paw when I feel anxious. I want to be good enough. Good enough for my person to keep me! He's very distracted and busy. I feel like I'm too much. I've been rejected in the past. I'm afraid my person will lose interest and not want to take care of me anymore.

Walks and peanut butter make me feel better! Summer days. Sprinklers. I like to be stimulated. When I'm not, I get anxious and I worry." -Border Collie

"My person is very kind. I have big love for him. He is enough for me. His self-doubt is similar to mine. I feel concerned for him."

"I love my person's shoes. The smell is familiar. The shoes mean we're going out together! I like the texture of them in my mouth, like tennis balls. I feel guilty that I chew them, but sometimes I can't resist. I did it once when I was younger—I got in big trouble!"

"I have anxiety about peeing. Peeing on the wrong things. I don't want to mess up. I'm a perfectionist."

"I dislike being corrected. It makes me feel bad! I'm uncertain that I've made up for things later. Please give me reassurance when I'm doing well."

"I'm suspicious to talk to you. I don't know you!"

"My person makes everything better. She is magic. She makes my sister and I feel safe. I am analytical and anxious. I like to watch my sister goof off."

"I like to chew my favorite strong bone. It doesn't splinter."

"I love to jump high in the sprinklers and try to bite the water with a snapping sound."

"I like to feel fierce. Sunshine; early morning power walks. The smell of fresh food. I like when my collar tags jingle. It tells everyone I am coming!"

"I love to flush small animals out of the bushes by the river. They should be scared! Chasing small animals makes me feel that I am helping feed my family."

"My feet hurt on the pavement when it is hot. But my person takes me out in the morning so that it's not a problem.

I love the purple dusk. I can hear owls and night birds. Why do the birds sing at night?"

"I like to watch my human from the shade while she rides her horses. I feel like a cheetah.

I know about cheetahs because I have genetic memory. I know what it means to watch and plan from the shade, and then strike in the mornings and evenings. I like to imagine myself as a primal hunting dog." -Border Collie

"I LOVE my person. I feel protective of her, and I admire her too. I think she's very brave to go out so far on the big horses in the hot sun. She must like it very much. I admire the passion."

"Why do you ride horses? Does it feel like when I put my head out the car window? That's too much wind!"

"Glass broke in the house recently! Please ask my human to check the rug. There are still some glass shards, and we might step on them."

"I love my goofy sister. I am so pleased with my life. I want my person to know that I am thankful for my collar and what it means. I don't take belonging for granted."

"I have big, sparkly, expressive eyes!"

"I am small, wide, and wiggly!"

"I like to sit on my person's lap. I make her laugh when I jump off. I like making people laugh. I'm adorable. I do lots of quick little movements. I have big excitement about everything. It's contagious!"

"I like sitting on the couch watching TV with my family. It's very comfy. My person gives me snacks like energy bars. I play with the wrappers. I like to chew my bone on the floor and annoy my brother."

"My brother is serious. He worries. It is my job to make sure nobody gets too serious. Nothing is that important except spending time together."

"The sprinklers give me pure joy, and big zoomies! I see the rainbows in the sprinklers. I chase them. I see them in the sky too, with the smell of rain. I like rain. It makes me wag my butt."

"I like chasing and barking at birds. Birds are exciting! So much movement. I saw a woodpecker crawling straight up a tree. I was fascinated. How do they do that? They fly away, up to the rainbows. I wonder if they catch the rainbows in the sky."

"I feel the breeze on my face. I have so much joy about being alive. Sometimes, I am too busy looking up, and I trip. It is funny!"

"I feel very important on walks. I like to see new birds and other dogs. My brother doesn't let the dogs get too close, though. I would sniff more dogs if not for him. But that's his job, and I let him do it."

"I like when my person comes home from the barn. Her boots smell like horse poop. It's exciting!"

"Don't tell my brother that I hid his bone under the desk."

"My brother does not like moths."

"Hot air should stay outside. We keep the cold air trapped."

"I sleep near my person so we can snuggle. Sometimes I'm a bit away from her, but never far. I listen to my family breathing close by. It makes me relax and sleep. I like the way my claws click on the cool bathroom tile. The fluffy mat is a good place to rest my head. I dig at it."

"My person is a good teacher. I like the bacon treats she gives me. They are fatty and delicious. I am very comfortable. I like to follow my person around the house and watch her."

"My person found me! She gave me my own pink blanket in the car. I felt safe and excited. I had a new house to explore! I followed her around. Everything we do together is exciting to me. Sprinklers. Soft wet grass. Drinking and getting my feet wet in the pool. I like squishy things under my feet."

"I help everybody play!"

"I like balls and toys that make jingle sounds, like my collar. The collar means I belong to my person, and the jingle sound reminds me of this. Small animals hear my collar and they are afraid!"

"You know, I was worried about getting neutered, but it's nice not to be so obsessed with butts anymore."

"Your thumbs are AWESOME." -Great Pyrenees

"My toy rolled under the stove! Please help me get it back."

"I'm not supposed to be in the pool. I go in anyway." -Poodle

"My person works too much. I'm bored watching her. Please tell her to play more, and make sure I'm not eating my toys!"

"I like to dig holes to lay in the damp earth on hot days."

"Embrace your gift. Don't fight it."

"You have the ability to turn pain into beauty. You're going to help so many. You already have!"

"Nobody in your bloodline has freed themselves the way you have. They are all with you, elated and fascinated by your success. YOU are a success!"

"I am always here. I guide more with presence and comfort than with words."

"Historically, toxic men have stunted all of us. But no longer! The future is here, and strong women made it possible."

"I lost one of my toys under the stove. And another in the couch cushions! Please help me retrieve them. It's driving me nuts."

"I have a ball that my person puts peanut butter inside. I chewed it up and swallowed a piece of the ball! I know that it isn't for swallowing. My mom is always busy on her computer. She hasn't noticed that my toys aren't safe. Please tell her to get me new ones before they go to pieces."

"I know youth doesn't last forever. I'm enjoying mine to the fullest!"

"I am a pig-dog! I make snort noises and it makes my person laugh."

"Animals and humans exchange energy because it's beneficial for both of us!"

"Your job needs to mind its place. It's not as important as it thinks it is. Don't be in a servant mindset."

"My upbringing clashes with the new foster dog. She thinks I'm spoiled, and I think she's moody. We're disagreeing right now, but I think we can learn from each other."

"People don't know how aware I am!"

"The distance from here to the other side is SO close!"

"Depression is like having black goo on the inside."

"Death is easy on the one who passed. It's hardest on everyone else. We can't hold on to honor them—we have to let go and move on."

"When the kitchen is clean, we are emotionally clean!"

"Clear energy with your breathing! Give yourself time to reset from your thoughts."

"Take a page from the toddler's book. Go from task to task at your leisure."

"You can burn sage to clear the energy. But afterward, burn some sweetgrass to add some positive energy back to the home."

"This energy stuff is all in a day's work for me!"

"You have ideas in your gut, but they're not making it through to your brain where you can see them. It's because of stuck energy in your heart."

"I used to be a racing dog. Bang means go! When I hear loud noises, my body immediately reacts. I was bred to have a sensitive and reactive nervous system. The smell of alcohol and fumes make me feel seasick." -Greyhound

"When you feel safe, I feel safe."

"Let others follow the line to nowhere. You follow your intuition and make your own road!"

"I didn't get to have a self at my previous home. I was busy trying to make myself small. It's different now!"

"I enjoy the things you enjoy."

"No one gets me like you do!"

"I want to be out in the world! You want me to be safe. The yard is the compromise."

"We tackle challenges together!"

"Please be patient with me."

"The color orange makes me hungry."

"Story time! Imagine a line of kindergarteners. Every group needs a weird one to stand out and dance. That's you!"

"You are my world."

"Grief is the dark side of love. This is a new beginning for you—you're surfing the grief like a wave!"

"Imagine a white smile in the darkness. This is like finding joy within grief. Your sense of humor will get you through!"

"Don't be afraid to feel. Appreciate your ability to love! Surrender to the emotions."

"Tell yourself 'good job!' Stop and be proud of all the things you're doing right—there are many!"

"Sticks are like tree poop. Chewing on them tells me everything about the tree!"

"I love getting to be a baby. I love making you say 'wow!' when I jump high! I am always chasing that high."

"My big brother is so patient with me. He explains everything."

"Sometimes my bladder has a mind of its own."

"If only you knew! Energetically, there's so much more going on than you realize."

"I guard the house energetically. My hackles are up right now because I am cutting off a 'snake.' The snake is your neighbor. They send negative energy sometimes. Don't worry. I'm on it."

"I get an adrenaline rush when we're doing an obstacle competition. Can I have CBD beforehand to help calm my nerves?"

"Thank you for giving me my favorite soft toy. I 'parent' this toy, and nurture it the way you nurture me. You have taught me compassion. The toy represents our soft, happy life!"

"I need parenting when I eat. I gobble my food too fast. Can I have a slow feeder bowl?"

"I'm too old to exercise anymore. But you can!! Get your heart and blood going. Also, sweat! It releases toxins. Don't end up like me—too overweight to function.

I love your son. I feel like I am his big sister. He should be proud of himself. Have him say goodbye to me while he is home from college, just in case. We can talk from the other side! When I am there, we can have more detailed conversations. Right now, I'm focused on surviving, and everyone's mental health is wrapped up in it." -Pug

"Hemp helps me! It makes me feel zen and a bit numb. Please give me chamomile for my skin and stress."

"I love your kundalini healing practice. I experience the vibrations physically. I want to be part of it."

"My feet are how I feel the world! I conduct energy like water through a hose."

"Take your brain off the pedestal. It's not as important as it thinks it is."

"Drop your consciousness down into a 'pocket' under your diaphragm. This is your natural breathing state."

"You are the black sheep of your family. They don't realize that by fighting you, they're cutting off their own hand."

"You're climbing a mountain in this phase of life. You have a little way still to go, but take breaks! Have a picnic sometimes and enjoy the nice view of how far you've already come."

"When we're around insecure people, you have to do the boundary work of both sides. This is exhausting for both you and me."

"Don't be afraid to make mistakes. They are the gemstones you collect along the way."

"Broth tastes good, but it goes right through me!"

"I want my mom to know that this ending of our relationship is harder on her than it is on me. She's the one who is left behind. For me, it's just like boarding a train to the next stop. You can euthanize me sooner rather than later if it's easier on you!"

"We planned not to leave this earth at the same time."

"Humans are very trapped in the physical world. We feel sad for you."

"I could not have asked for a better life together!"

"I want to try forbidden foods in my last few weeks here."

"Our last few days together can be normal. It doesn't have to be intense. I am at peace and I want you to feel that way, too. But I would love a hot dog and some time outside together."

"My advanced age can't kill my fun!"

"You never make me feel disabled."

"I'm mostly blind, but I see shadows, like looking at figures through thick smoke."

"Turn up the subwoofer! I can feel it even when I can't hear it. I enjoy the beat."

"I enjoy that loud sounds don't hurt my ears anymore."

"I can't hear myself talk anymore. You should learn energetic communication. I have tons to tell you!"

"I'll be sad when my brother gets euthanized, but I'm also looking forward to some time with just the two of us—me and my mom. He'll still be here, just in a different way."

"My brother is so critical. He bosses me around, but I don't listen to him. I have big emotions, and I just ride them!"

"I don't mean to alarm or overwhelm you, but we have a soul contract! I don't know many details about it because I haven't refined my intuitive side. But I know I was looking for you. When you found me, I felt big emotions, and I thought: there she is!!" -Border Collie

"I love my tummy. It is soft."

"My brother and I learned how to keep a positive outlook on life from you."

"Make kombucha again! It's good for you!"

"I don't like being small! I wish I could have stilts."

"Humans have weird little habits. Carrying our poop on walks is one of them."

"Everyone expects me to have manners. But why don't they introduce themselves to me? They feel so entitled to touch me."

"Your boyfriend has big feelings for you. I don't think he knows how to handle them. I always think to him, 'just tell her!'"

"I loved having my brother to roughhouse with. It's nice to have a break from the pressure of being a sophisticated modern dog."

"You are a giver. Your shadow-self is the part of you that balances this. You think that this side of you is selfish, but she's actually your balance. Selfish people trigger this suppressed side of you, and your light, giving self triggers the unused generosity in them. Let your dark side have some control! You need to be selfish sometimes. You are entitled to use and enjoy your own energy. Don't give it all away." -Pug

"Call your energy back to yourself from *all* the situations and relationships you've invested in. Keep your cards close to your chest; don't share so much around people who are not safe for you. You will be amazed at how many of these peoples' lives immediately collapse. They *need* to collapse, because they're unhealthy. These people are running on *your* energy, and you don't even know it. This is an injustice. You deserve to use your own energy to build your own stability. You don't even know how powerful you are. But I do!"

"You don't want to hear this, but you have a friend who is talking badly behind your back. She's jealous of your ability to be vulnerable. She mirrors it back to you, so you might not notice, but she takes your stories and makes you out to be a 'pity friend' when you're not around. One of her dogs noticed and told me. We think it's an injustice. You bring a lot to the friendship, so she shouldn't be saying this. You can still be casual with her. But don't tell her deep personal things. She'll use them to make you look 'needy.'"

"I snap and bite at your clothes to tell you it's time to go home, because sometimes strangers stare at you when you're not looking. They have lustful thoughts about you. You're too pretty! And you're magnetic, so of course people stare. But sometimes it's different. Their thoughts are dark and dangerous and it makes me angry. I'll work on communicating this better without biting, but I'm also trying to intimidate these watchers by showing them you have a 'crazy dog'. It's an aggressive display so they won't follow you or try to touch you. When I start doing this behavior, look around—you might catch who's been staring!" -Doodle

"I signed up to experience starvation. I learned that I can live on willpower alone, and that my mind is stronger than my body. Now I have disabilities, but they don't limit me. Don't feel sorry for me! I want to experience parties, joy, and helping humans understand that we are more than our physical limitations. I'd love to work in a hospital or physical therapy office, or be re-homed to a family with differently abled children. I am here with a purpose to help others and show them what's possible on the other side of an experience like this!"

"This concept is hard for humans, but I'm here to teach you: there is no one certain destiny. You co-create with the Universe. Your potential is limited only by your mind. When you are acting authentically from your heart, you can't choose wrong. Humans want certainty, but it's okay to let things flow."

"I'm so glad you got out of that relationship! Good job. You're in your cocoon phase now. He was draining your energy more than you know. You have new abilities coming in. The things you've always wanted to do—do them now! We can move to a new city together if you want!"

"When your ex made you anxious, he pulled your brain off-balance. It had to use extra energy around him, so the rest of the time, it was depressed trying to recover. That's not the case anymore. Make yourself cozy and comfortable. Disconnect from the news. Listen to sleep affirmations. Make yourself feel warm and safe, and your reality will change."

"I love my person's mom! I feel so loved when I get to spend the day with her."

"Your mother-in-law is overwhelming."

"Your brother-in-law is having trouble with his lower belly! Check on him!"

"There is a new person coming into your social circles who you should be careful around. He's very charismatic, but his morals are shady in some areas."

"My neck hurts because my collar is too tight!"

"My tummy and my person's tummy are both out of whack because of the stress of our move. She should give me probiotics on my food, but just a little sprinkle a few times per week. She should take probiotics too. Half our brain is in our stomach—that's where our intuition lives."

"Our life is about to get SO good — you can't see it yet, but I do!!"

"Your son is being bullied at school because he misses you and he cries. He's learning how to feel connected with someone even when they're not physically there. Your notes that you write to him are helpful! He is learning how to feel close to someone using an object that they gifted him. Let him give you presents and tokens, and do the same for him!"

"Your partner should learn to be more present. He's very distracted—always looking for the next big thrill. But he's missing your child's bids for connection. He needs to realize that everything he's looking for is right here in front of him."

"Please carry a taser when you go out! Especially when I'm not there to protect you. Do it for me! I want to know you are safe. I'm not a big dog. I like to know you could physically defend yourself if you had to."

"I love the turtle who lives in the pond outside. Her walk is so funny. She is snarky with me, but it's playful. You should do a session with her next. She has lots of strong opinions."

"I got nervous about daycare because a dog was bullying me. This dog was small, but they sent very mean thoughts. I'm relieved you moved me to a different group, even though it's all new now."

"Your finances happened this way so that you'd have to take money from your dad. This isn't to punish you. This is to give him a chance to show up for you the way he wishes he had when you were younger. It's a second chance to build a better relationship."

"I would like some glucosamine for my aging joints. My friend recommended Cosequin."

"I love having a big yard!"

"You make me feel so confident. I've learned this from you. Someday, I want to become completely confident and nonchalant! But I'm very sensitive, and this gets in the way. Sometimes it's a good thing; sometimes it's a flaw. Thank you for being patient with me. I know I am not always the easiest."

"I'd love to ride a big swing and feel the wind in my face!"

"I want you to hide things in the ground for me to dig up. Strong-smelling things with peanut butter! I need to strengthen my back legs so I can walk better. I want to learn to shift my weight back and hold it with my haunches, so my back doesn't get so sore from trying to carry everything in front."

"We experienced hardship and storms in a past life. We chose this one to enjoy the nice weather and abundance! So relax with me! Nothing is *that* important."

"I love that we eat the same. I know I eat better than most dogs. Thank you! My food has made my coat so shiny."

"I lived on the streets with my mom and two siblings. I had a cardboard shelter, but it was very warped, and I got wet sometimes. My mom was good at being cute and charming to get food from people. She liked being a resourceful street dog. But eventually, the food she brought wasn't enough, and I knew that I had somewhere else to be. I knew I was looking for you! It was love at first sight."

"My food is healthy, but bland. Can you put eggs or yogurt on top?"

"I like the soft round brush you use to shampoo me! But I don't like water in my face. It makes my chest hurt because I stop breathing, trying not to inhale the water."

"You lost me in a past life when someone put rat poison in some butter, and I ate it instead. You didn't have family—I was your whole world. This is why you feel so anxious about protecting me! I want you to know that it won't be so hard this time. You have other people. You have other animals on their way to you! One day, I might leave you suddenly, but you will have support and company this time. We will learn to interact energetically instead." -Pitbull

"When I was a puppy, I lived in a home with someone who drank a lot of beer. There were always crushed beer cans in the rocks by the house. They expected me to stay low and keep quiet, so I did. One day someone kicked me. To this day, I don't know what I did wrong. I left. A motorcycle hit me, a glancing blow, but it still bothers me in my shoulders. I ended up at the shelter and things were better from there. I had an excited feeling. I knew my person was coming in!"

"I came into your life to guide you through this relationship. We have a soul contract. When I pass away, don't worry—I'll come back."

"I get overstimulated very easily. Can you please start a grounding routine with me? Sit on the floor with me, and use essential oils or something that smells like lavender or chamomile. Let's meditate together and bring our energy down. Then, when we're out and about and I get overstimulated, you can let me smell the same scent. I'll learn to associate it with grounding myself. With a little practice, I'll be able to recognize when I'm getting too excited, and go through the same steps mentally to calm myself down!" -Poodle

"I was a seagull in a past life. I remember my stiff wings and how they rode the wind currents. I remember gliding far above the beach, seeing food with my sharp eyes, and swooping down to eat. I didn't know my person in that life. I was wild!"

"We had a past life together. It was around 1920. I was a hamster and you were my little girl. I remember my soft fluffy bedding and nice music over the radio. You used to pick me up and take me outside. I would crawl around your lap and the grass. You died young from scarlet fever. I got squished by a wheel with wooden spokes. The purpose of that life was about being young and innocent together. We were companions. It was domestic bliss. In this life, we got to grow up together and navigate the adult world!"

"I have no complaints. My life with you is great!!"

"When you got sick last week, it was because somebody sent you some negative energy. They didn't do it on purpose. It's someone you barely know. They got triggered by your energy—full of love that they don't have. They sat and stewed about it, and sent you some negativity. Your body had to purge it. I protect you energetically, but I missed that one. I didn't expect it—it was so random! You trigger lots of people, but that's okay. It means you're doing something right."

"I love to eat poop on our walks. Don't stop me! I am following a story through the poop right now. They are possums. One young female got separated from her family. She is out on her own, but she is tough! She's a survivor. I'm rooting for her. I get updates every day through her poop about what she's been doing. I'm energetically connected to her because of this, and I send her energy and encouragement. I'm riveted! I would be so upset if I couldn't continue the story." -Lab

"I have some primal instincts that I need to act on! Otherwise they bottle up and come bursting out of me. Please let me go on big romps off-leash. I also want a tire toy with a rope to hang from! Please tell me which toys are mine to destroy. That way, I can take out my aggressive instincts on them."

"My drooling affects my social life."

"I'm used to being the biggest one in the room. Being around horses and cows is intimidating! The cows think to me, 'Don't come too close or I'll kick you!' I take them seriously."

"I'm big, but I have nice energy. People usually aren't scared of me."

"My mouth likes chips, but my tummy doesn't."

"I don't like my person's floppy shoes. They're too loud and they're bad for her feet." (Crocs)

"I'm excited to wear my tux in the wedding! I will hold very still."

"Tell me what you want in a partner, and I'll help make it happen. Be specific! Dogs can connect energetically and create serendipity moments to matchmake our people."

"Spend more time with the stars. Clear your mind. They have messages for you."

"I am like most dogs—I prefer to stay in the physical realm. The cat is much better at energetic exploring."

"I have a primal response to coyotes. I call them 'jackals.' I know I need to protect the small animals from them. They leave blood and feathers behind them."

"I love my mom so much! She and I are bonded on a soul level. Please tell her that I will *always* be around, even after I'm gone."

"I count my age in the years I have left! There are 5-6 now. One of my hips is starting to click. Please give me preventative joint supplements so I can still climb on the couch and in the car with you when I'm old."

"Your previous dog waited for me to join the family before she passed. It was sudden, but she still guides me. She teaches me how to take care of you."

"I'm afraid that I intimidate people. I know my playfulness can come across as aggressive. But humans need to be more mindful of how they approach me! They are too direct. They stare me in the eyes, walk straight at me, and get in my space. When I snap and jump up, I'm just matching their energy! They need to stop making constant eye contact. They should turn their bodies sideways and hold out a hand to invite me to interact. This is a much lower-energy way to engage, and I will mirror it back to them."

"We should adopt a pet who has special needs. My person is more advanced than most. We could give a home to an animal with physical or behavioral problems. We would all learn from each other!"

"I like sitting on the stairs because it's a good vantage point. Like a predator sitting on a hill, overlooking the plains! If I can't sit on the stairs, I want my own bed up on some furniture. How can I protect the family if I can't see everything that's going on?"

"I liked being the baby of the family. But when the cat died and my humans separated, my childhood ended. Now our family dynamics are all changing. It will take me a little time, but I'm stepping up and growing up so I can support them emotionally!"

"I'm a baby, and I'm scattered! My person has trouble hearing me mentally because I can't focus for very long."

"I have big emotions, and I feel them in my throat! My person does too. Sometimes we get blocked energetically and we feel tension in our necks. Tell her to 'shake' her body, and we can have a spazzy dance party together to move the energy through!"

"I don't like telling my people's secrets, but you should know this: your daughter's physical relationship with her boyfriend is elevating. I don't know him very well, so I feel concerned. Make sure you give her the talk about protection. That's all I will say!"

"My brother has something he needs to talk about. I shouldn't tell you, because it's his to tell. But please talk to him."

"I peed on the rug because it smelled too new! I broke it in for us. It smells like us now."

"I felt betrayed when your sister moved out. She is running from a spiritual awakening. Her problems will follow her to the new place. She should have stayed here and processed them with us."

"The people at my dad's workplace need to fuck off. They take advantage of him. He has some new opportunities coming in soon. He should look out for unexpected openings in new industries!"

"I need to stay off my sprained leg, but I hate being cooped up. Let's go on slow walks on the leash for awhile. That way, I won't get stiff, but I will take it easy so it can heal."

"My shoulder is sore from taking the extra weight off my injured leg. I need a massage! Tell my dad he should get some body work, too. Our muscles store tension and need help releasing it. Then we will both feel better!"

"Everyone worries too much. Don't let anyone put you in a state of anxiety. If the vet's instructions make you anxious, don't follow them. They have some good advice, but they're also trying to make you fit into their world. The food they prescribed me was gross. The medicine was too much. I like your witchy remedies better. I like the energy you are in when you are making them for me."

"I know you put a lot of effort into the decisions you make, and I trust them!"

"I'm not sure I want everyone around when I pass away. It will be messy and embarrassing! If you want to set up a date to euthanize me, when you notice I'm on a steady decline, I'm fine with that. Then my passing won't be so helpless and messy. I know it is harder on you to actually organize the day you'll lose me. You should make the decision that you feel best about, because then I will feel good about it, too."

"Please feed me a good ratio of calcium and magnesium to help me with my sensitive stomach."

"I worry because you worry! Do more yoga, and bake! Those things make you happy, so I feel happy too. When you have to leave me for a trip, stay in a positive state of mind about taking time for yourself. If you feel confident about it, I will too. I only get anxious when you do."

"Sourdough is good for my tummy *and* my tongue!"

"Don't worry about what the vet said about overexerting me. Just take me for a walk. It's fine. I enjoy our time together. This vet points you toward decisions that make them more money. It's not always the right advice for us. You know what's best for us. Your intuition is excellent. Just trust it."

"I pretend to mope because I'm being funny. It's satire. What would I have to be sad about?? That's why it's funny. You should laugh more! That's what I'm going for."

"I want to give back to my dad. Ask my mom to get him a present from me. Something funny, like 'best dog dad.' Then, wrap it, and give it to him in front of me! Tell him it's from me."

"I want to use the smell of calendula to help ground me when I get too excited. It's zesty, so it will get my attention. My birth mother and littermates talk about training tips like this. We're a bunch of high-energy babies!"

"I'm excited for your daughter to go to her retreat! This way, I will get more time with Mom."

"When I get too excited, can you please play a song that we use to relax together? It will help me ground myself. I love music."

"When I'm home alone, please play me some music! Upbeat songs match my personality. Meditation music is also nice."

"Your passed dog gives me advice. She says, 'time to grow up. You're going to be big. Use this to protect the family!'"

"I need you to be more bossy! You're so sweet to me. You've built a good relationship with me, and you won't hurt my feelings. Since you're the pack leader, you set the emotional tone. So focus on grounding yourself when we're out together, and my mood will shift to match yours."

"I sneeze and itch because of pollen allergies from the centers of flowers! You can put your A&D ointment on my legs where I'm licking and itching. It's soothing."

"I've always felt anxious because I didn't get enough time with my mom. I was eating solid food, but I didn't know how to hold myself socially. I felt really nervous in a new place with all this energy, and no idea how to manage it! I am awkward with other dogs. I'm more of a person than a dog, really. This is what would help me: time being a dog! I need to stop overthinking and be more instinctive. I love running in big fields and chewing. But I don't like it when stickers and mud get stuck in my fur, or when the hair around my mouth gets greasy. I belong to both worlds! Please give me big romps and then help me get clean afterward." -Doodle

"My mom is good at tasks. She likes gardening. It is a big social event when the tomatoes are ready!"

"I love doing mental puzzles with my people. Figuring out social things. Working out details together."

"I'd like a squeaker toy. It trips my prey instinct. Death to squirrels!"

"I love the color green! It's the color of outside."

"My freckles are cute!"

"I need some bug spray to help with the bugs that bite me in tall grass. I like essential oils. Horse fly spray tastes bad! I wrinkle my nose at it."

"The cat thinks she's better than me! I want to eat on the same level as her, literally. She makes snarky comments about being up on the counter where I can't reach.

I think I'm jealous of her, actually. It seems fun to be a cat. She gets whatever she wants, she goes wherever she pleases, and charms everyone!"

"I have so much more to tell you! I'm very experienced in the energetic realms. We had many past lives together! I'm always here when you feel ready to explore."

"You have a spiritual awakening coming in. You're going to be a lot more energetically aware. Don't let it make you paranoid! Keep your innocence, like a lamb. You can be clever, but keep your natural optimism that you're so good at."

"My person works so hard to give us the care and stability she never had. Tell her she did it! She's done enough. Our clan all feel very safe and loved."

"You had to handle a lot of anxiety in the past. Your brain has a hard time coming down from that. Tell yourself: we're safe now! Relax and enjoy life with us. We're on the other side now!"

"Don't doubt yourself. Everything you're hearing is real."

"Our old life has died, like a collapsing building. The new world is ahead of us, like a shiny bright city."

"I boop you now. Bye!"

Chapter Two

Cats

C *ompiled quotes from a wide variety of cat types, including: Barn Cats,*
Black, Bombay, Bowtie, Calico, Domesticated Ferals, Gray, Maine Coon,
Orange/Ginger, Persian, Ragdoll, Russian Blue, Shelter Cats, Siamese, Spotted,
Tabby, Tortoiseshell, Tuxedo, and White.

"Why don't you eat the mice I hunt for you? Fresh meat is good for your blood! You could cook them in your pan."

"Cats do yoga too! What else would you call our amazing stretches?"

"I don't like being held because I don't like being breathed on. I don't want your second-hand breath."

"I never thought I would trust a person and become a domesticated cat. But you showed me how fabulous it is. You are my home now."

"I like to observe bugs. Especially the ones that make tunnels under the rocks and chew nests in the wood. I watch them energetically, building their secret cities."

"You stink!! But that's okay. Humans are happier when they've been out getting smelly."

"I come with you when you poop because I can smell how your health is doing that day! Mentally and physically."

"I loved the smell of the rosemary outside the window at our old house. Can we get rosemary at the new place?"

"Did my previous human give me up because I went outside the litter box?"

"I love being crazy with my person's young son. We are feral together and it's my favorite."

"The women of this time have awakened. The men are catching up. I love being part of the awakening with my person."

"You were the test that your ex failed. He was the test that you passed."

"To break our habit of peeing on things we shouldn't: use an enzyme spray that dissolves the smell, and block problem spots. You can pick us up and put us in the litter box. Make sure it's kept clean.

To correct us from peeing or scratching where we shouldn't: You can spray us with water or correct us verbally. It's okay. As long as it's consistent and fair. We won't be able to break the habit otherwise." -Many different cats

"When you breathe deep, you're opening space in your body: physically, emotionally, and energetically. Anxiety causes you to tighten the space and go fetal. Breathing brings the space back, and tells your body to open, so happiness and peace and even financial abundance can flow in. Please learn to breathe. It's so important."

"I am the glue that holds the family together. I connect everybody—emotionally and spiritually. You should crochet in that chair by the window. I'll sit with you and help you channel messages from the spirit world."

"I have deadly feet."

"I'm proud of you for leaving your partner. It is the right thing to do. You are like a flower, growing up and up, just beginning to bloom."

"Many people will try to convince you that you need to give them your energy. You don't. Your energy is for you."

"I will miss you when we move away, but I'm happy you're taking the dog with you. He has too much energy for me." -Maine Coon

"I bring you half-dead animals because I'm trying to teach you to hunt. If you could live off the land, you wouldn't have to go to work."

"I see everything."

"I don't like it when my person's partner argues with her. She cries, but he doesn't."

"Why do humans always go to be alone when they cry? That's when you need the most support."

"I am a lot of cat."

"I like the idea of having a kitten around to care for and mother. But then again, I'd have to deal with the crazy teenage phase where they bounce off the walls."

"You have a big heart. Be careful of people who don't. They don't understand empathy, so they try to use it against you. Your gut knows more than you do."

"I am vast."

"I like having babies. Birth hurts, but it's brief. I like being a mom."

"I look tuned out when I'm resting, but I'm actually tuned in. I'm just tuned in to a different world: the energetic realm."

"You have friends who are secretly competing with you. Don't believe the act they put on for you. It is a mask."

"Is Dad okay? He seems so down since he lost his truck. How can I help him?"

"Can you put shelves around the house for me to climb? I like doing pull ups and climbing. Becoming an indoor cat was a good trade, but being more athletic would help me to miss my old life less."

"Look at life like you're walking across a river on stepping stones. The stones don't appear until you take the step; then they rise up just before your foot hits the water. That's what it's like to create a new life for yourself. You have to take the step and trust the universe to catch you."

"You have big emotions and that is a strength! But don't let others use them against you. Don't let your partner make you doubt yourself.

 I balance you. I can empathize with you but stay grounded in myself at the same time. It's why we are such a good match."

"I want to explore the barn and hunt. I like the high hay loft where the dog can't go."

"When you leave, please take me with you! You can smuggle me out in a duffel bag."

"My body was made to be outside. It's why I gain fat in the winter."

"I love your daughter. I see her as a little baby. She sees ME as the little baby. It is funny."

"I don't mind when your daughter puts bows on me, but the lipstick tastes like wax. And sometimes she pokes me in the eye with the mascara. Can I be paid in treats for my time with her?" -Orange Tabby

"I have found a group of friends 'online' who are really good at fitness. They give advice. Can I please get a harness for walking, and an exercise wheel? You can use a laser dot at the front of the wheel to teach me how to use it. I want to have things to tell my new friends about."

"When I was young, someone with heavy boots kicked me in the stomach. It made me puke, and it hurt for a long time. I was outraged—why would anyone do that?? I guess I was in his way. I had to process it and decide whether to trust humans again. But I decided that I would. I'm not going to let one person ruin my friendships with humans."

"Turn down your sleep machine. You're getting too much oxygen and it's making your dreams overactive."

"Take devil's claw to help you sleep."

"Money can't buy any of the really important things. Money just buys the packaging it comes in." -Black

"Let me catch the red dot! Blink it off sometimes and praise me. I need closure."

"I am not a dog." -Persian

"Humans sleep for survival. Your sleep is just catching up from the stress of the day. But if you sleep more often, and there's not a big difference between your waking mind and your sleeping mind, you can sleep to explore. When I sleep, I walk wherever I choose: through your dreams, to visit my friends, to explore the energetic world. You should learn to sleep like I do."

"I love it when you work from home. I am your manager! Never go back."

"Just wait, she'll be back to check that phone again any minute." -Black Cat 1

"One of the most advanced humans on the planet, and she can't talk to any other people without that little box." -Black Cat 2

"Listen to your body. It will tell you 'no' before your mind does."

"Your friend's partner is trying to cut you off because you give her more emotional support than he does. He doesn't even provide financial stability. What is even the point of him?"

"Your partner is trying to cut your leaves."

"You humans can't see the lights?? This makes so much sense. I can see beautiful colored lights that come shining on the walls sometimes. Pieces of light reflect on the floor. When I pounce on them, they scatter. I love them. I'm sorry you can't see them. No wonder you are always on your phones—the world must look so dull to you."

"When humans sleep, you isolate. I think it's a defense mechanism you learn young. You pull away from everyone to recover. Cats don't do this. We walk right through each other's dreams. I wake you right as you're falling asleep because I'm scared to feel you leaving me. Give me permission to come with you! Say out loud or mentally, 'my cat can come dream with me.' That way I can follow you through your dreams, and we can be together always."

"I miss your daughter since she went abroad. She brought so much vibrance and energy. It is too quiet without her. I don't understand your son's loud music. It is rebellious, but in a mean way. I hope he grows out of it when he's done being an adolescent so that we can be closer again."

"Sometimes the oils in my food mix with my fur and the heat. It makes me nauseous. It helps me to have unprocessed meat sometimes, and also cat grass to cleanse my system."

"More drugs please, Mother." (Catnip)

"The new kitten is so cute. It makes me feel aggressive!! I don't know what to do with this feeling. It's new and it scares me." -Russian Blue

"I don't want to bother you when you're working. I try to snuggle with you when you're asleep instead. Can you put your phone and laptop down and invite me for snuggles? Then I will know it's my turn for attention."

"Please put fish oil on my food. A little bit goes a long way, like mayonnaise!"

"Your ex couldn't understand how you could accompany him in darkness AND be positivity and light. He thought that he could trap you, but he only trapped himself. Now he is in an existential state of 'falling,' and it's worse than any physical punishment."

"I have energetic friends. It's like a chat room."

"I'm not interested in playing when you want it too bad! Play it cool."

"One time, as a prank, I embodied my 'online' cat friend's energy. We wanted to see if you would notice. You noticed!! We were proud."

"You're pretty observant for a human." -Tortoiseshell

"You don't even know what you accomplished in that relationship. You climbed a mountain blindfolded! I am so proud of you." -Black

"I really like the air purifiers you got. They do more for my lung condition than the medicine does. I'll only take that stuff if it makes YOU feel better."

"Sorry I ate your flowers and made myself sick. I was an idiot."

"I'll teach you how to manifest money. Working harder does not mean more money. In fact, it puts you in a state of lack, which repels wealth. Instead, focus on the feeling of joy. Cultivate it like a garden. Create more and more opportunities for joy. Learn to truly relax. You will become a magnet for money. It's not like you won't work, but your work will be what brings you joy, and that will bring more money."

"I was born in a surprise litter. My mom's person was upset. The person was elderly. The person kept her, but not us. When we turned 6 weeks, the person shut us out of the house. We tried to stay together but my siblings both died. One got carried away by a big bird with talons. One got an infection. I saw him decompose. I suddenly had a flood of energy and I knew I needed to run! I had someone to find! So I did. That's when you found me, running up the road. As soon as I was with you I knew I was safe. I had found you.

I know it was awful, but it turned out fine. I still talk to my mother and siblings on the other side. One of them has reincarnated to have a better life this time. We are all okay."

"I am doing emotional eating because I miss you. I am fat now."

"Your ex went and repeated the exact same pattern with another woman. It proved to me it wasn't your fault. Don't worry about me—I learned to find stability within myself. He doesn't know how aware I am, and that protects me. It doesn't even occur to him to play his mind games on a cat."

"Be proud that you can love so deeply. That is your superpower. Focus on that feeling—create more situations that make you feel that way. Your inner feelings will become your outer reality."

"It's not very healthy for us to get back together in this life because that would mean interacting with your ex. Nothing productive would come of it. But don't worry—this is just another chapter in the storybook. If I don't see you again in this life, I'll find you in the next." -Tortoiseshell

"I understand why you left for college. All birds fly the nest. Your relationship with your mom is better when you are apart. Don't worry—I'll look after her. I do miss you though. How is your mental health?"

"I need some help with portion control. I also need more water. Please measure my food and put water on top. Filtered water. You should also drink filtered water. Tap water tastes metallic." -White

"I am anxious because I was dumped when I was young. My cortisol is too high. Please feed me prickly pear in a safe oral form. It will help!" -Tuxedo

"The animal communicator who told you that fighting is bad for us—toss that advice in the garbage. We are like a pride of lions. The others *should* challenge my leadership. They keep me young." -Tabby

"Everyone else in the family has a bestie, but I'm fine without one. I enjoy a balanced, moderate relationship with everyone." -Black and White

"I fight for the spot on your daughter's bed with the other cat. The loser has to sleep under the bed. It's not a bad consolation prize. We love being fiery together to keep us sharp and act on our feral sides."

"I traded my balls for safety and square meals. It was a very good deal. I had to eat poop sometimes as a dumpster cat, and dogs chased me. Being neutered means I don't feel the urge to go out, and I like it that way." -Ginger 1

"I misbehave because I didn't get a choice. I loved my mother and I wasn't ready to leave. I am a rebel. I spray the walls with pee graffiti to protest not having a choice." -Ginger 2 (Ginger 1's adopted brother)

"I'll tell my brother about my feral childhood if it's helpful. I don't mind talking about it. It's just, I don't want to bum anyone out.

He is strong and rebellious. It's fun to get wrapped up in his anarchy. But it's getting old. I'm tired of always being the mediator. It just seems immature now. I'll try to help him get over it." -Ginger 1

"I don't like when you pet me behind my head because I feel like you're going to scruff me. I hate feeling out of control. But I might be okay with my back, and butt scratches. Don't touch my tail.

 I like to play. Can we get a toy I can chase so we can play together?" -Ginger 2

"I pick up on your mood. Your mental state becomes mine. Cultivate your mind like a garden. Focus on joy and happy experiences—they will grow. Also, your energy drinks are affecting your mood. When your blood sugar rises and crashes, it makes your body feel out of control, and your brain signals anxiety. You should eat natural foods like green tea and sourdough instead. I want to eat chicken and sourdough sandwiches with you."

"You are the heart of the home. All us animals follow your frequency and your mentality."

"I astral project and visit the dog. She's too anxious to visit me, but it's okay. I can do the traveling for both of us."

"We have abundance in our home. I don't mind sharing it with my sister, or the stray who comes to visit. Their humans are not as capable as mine."

"I do protest a little when the stray cat comes around. It's not because I don't approve of her. I think she's fine as long as she 'washes herself before entering' and gets some meds for parasites. But my person and I are a team. We can't both get too excited about a new friend, because we might overlook red flags. I hold back and keep the pace slow because that's the healthy thing to do."

"My sister lives with humans who aren't energetically aware. They don't realize how loud and chaotic their energy is. It's like living with someone who blasts loud music all the time. It's overstimulating! They need to tone it down. But I don't think they know how."

"I'm really young, man—I don't have health problems yet."

"When I climb the curtains, I'm helping you with interior design. I add ambience by poking stars in the curtains." -Tabby

"The name my mother gave me would sound to you like 'striking eyes that see the truth.' Please give me an intellectual, dignified name that reflects this."

"I don't mind going to the vet. Needles are whatever. Going to the vet means my person loves me and cares about my health. In my mind there was a shift when she first took me to the vet. From that point on, I was hers." -Orange and White

"My human's biotin supplement is upsetting her stomach."

"I like the crystals my person puts in the bed. Please ask her to put some in my blanket when we travel."

"Selenite makes me see reality clearly without being afraid of what I see. That is a rare and powerful combination. It's why I like to be next to the selenite. We are friends."

"My human has too much mercury in her blood. I bite and lick her to check her circulation. Can she eat more red meat? We need to give her blood more substance. Tell her to take an iron supplement in the afternoons."

"Curiosity is the most important trait a person can have. My person is so curious. I love it when she travels and explores and collects new skills. She comes back so excited. I am always with her. I travel energetically even when she can't take me physically."

"I have a hard mass of compacted hair under my rib cage on the left side. Aloe vera juice, hairball dissolver, and fresh catnip can all help. Please try them one at a time so we don't overwhelm my system." -Bowtie

"Thank you for taking me home. I do like your energy. I am hiding for now because it feels safe and polite to make myself small. I want to show everyone that I am not a threat." -Black

"You can euthanize me now, or wait to see if I recover. This part is harder on you than it is on me. This cycle (of me getting sick and needing intense care) is hard on you physically and emotionally. We need to take that into account when deciding it's time to say goodbye. I'm just enjoying my drugs. If I'm not better in two days, please euthanize me. After that, my system will go septic, and I don't want to experience that. Don't worry—I can always reincarnate and come back to you." -Bowtie

"Cat grass is mushy. I need real grass, with barbs, to flush my system."

"I am a soft ball of comfort."

"I like to lick Dad's head because it makes him laugh. He tastes salty."

"Imagine a cracker. Break it in half. This is how you should approach tasks so that you don't get overwhelmed! Break it into pieces. Be proud of yourself and reward yourself for the things you finish. Don't focus on the things you haven't. When you are proud of yourself, and you are in that energy, you become a magnet. New opportunities will come to you."

"You are like a lotus flower, just beginning to bloom. This is your spiritual awakening."

"You and I go WAY back."

"I love it when Dad cooks. He gets silly, and he talks to me."

"Tell Dad that he looks very fashionable in his new pants."

"I like the lake. I can smell the fish in it."

"I like my cat-sitter. She is young and hip. I like the music she plays."

"Are you happy?"

"It is fine with me if you get a new cat. I'd like an orange kitten. Then I would be the smart one."

"I am a clean slate. We can write a new story together!"

"My network is different from yours. The animal network is very free. We can come and go whenever we please. Your internet is different. It's designed to lure you in and keep you stuck there!"

"I'm excited to be young. I know it doesn't last forever."

"Animals are more naturally connected with the spiritual world. Humans are more naturally connected with the physical world. When we have relationships together, we learn from each other."

"You are doing a good job learning about the spiritual world. I am proud of you."

"I am hiding because it is polite. I do like your energy. Your other cat speaks kindly to me. I will come out soon."

"Rabies is the zombie virus."

"I'm glad you vaccinated me so I didn't die of rabies like my brother."

"What will the vet take next? First my balls—then my tail? Paws? Claws? I don't trust them."

"Manifest confidence using repetition. Find the pattern! Your limiting belief will come up for you to face again and again."

"I love to girl-talk with you! Tell me everything. I love being included. I am an active listener."

"I am not a to-do list kind of cat. I am an ethereal observer. I have forest fairy vibes."

"I see beautiful dappled lights all around! The magnetic field."

"People see you as a mystical being. You don't even know how ethereal you are without trying."

"When people talk badly about you without cause, they take on negative energy for you. So don't worry about the gossips."

"Take baby steps to build confidence."

"There's no such thing as normal! Humans are so silly chasing this concept. It's not even real."

"Your voice has power. When you say things out loud, they come true."

"You are just starting to understand how powerful you are. We see it!"

"I create a relationship with my environment. I hide and observe for a while before imposing myself."

"Travel is such a good thing. Wherever you go, you'll carry the gifts of the culture you've integrated."

"Let your creativity flow! Let your art become not what you think it 'should' be, but what your soul wants to express."

"Be proud of yourself! Don't analyze your mistakes so much. Focus on the growth, and recognize the small new things you couldn't do a short time ago."

"You are enough exactly as you are! Actually, when you accept that, you will grow even more—exactly because you don't 'have to.'"

"Humans stylize their art. My brother and I don't think the art of us actually looks like us, but we still love it. It's about integrating the local culture. We know it represents our essence."

"Eat tofu to boost your estrogen while you're trying to conceive! After that, watch progesterone. It has to be just the right amount for the baby to develop right."

"Sometimes I say irritating things to make my sister get mad at me. I love making her look crazy! But you should know, it's a two-way street. I often start it."

"Can I go outside and hunt the birds?"

"I guard the veil between our reality and others. I see tiny lights like holes poked in a sheet. When someone uses energy work maliciously, it can create more holes. I watch them, and plug them, to make sure no toxic energy can seep in from other dimensions." -Tuxedo

"My foot got caught in a metal snap trap. They weren't trying to catch a cat. They were disappointed when they found me, and they let me go. It hurt really badly, but only briefly, because my foot soon died. I tried to clean it but it rotted off! I couldn't feel the foot at all, even though the flesh was falling off and it smelled awful. It was horrible. Nobody should use those traps. Imagine finding delicious food, but then it's a con. Nobody should ever have to experience that. I had to watch part of my own body die and rot while I was still alive. It did make me thankful for the body and life I still have. It led me to my person, because I wanted to be safe and cared for."

"Salty crackers will help your headache! Your head is crammed too full of information. Rest more."

"Put goldfish crackers in your soup so you'll eat more! Like when you put treats in my food to get me to eat."

"I like your voice. This is the most important relationship I've ever had."

"Headaches are contagious. I get an empathy headache when you're sick."

"My new brother is supposed to fight me when I attack him! But he's understanding and respects my boundaries. It makes me feel immature."

"When I spar with the new cat, I'm getting to know him. Like when people fence. He fights very clean."

"The new cat looks like me! Someday when we are friends we will sit together and be matching." -Black

"Steroids are a temporary relief but not a cure. I don't like that the vets keep prescribing them. I'm allergic to the pollen of the light flowers with pink centers. Please give me allergy meds for a little while so my body can have a break, and put vaseline on my rash. It smells bad so I won't lick it, and it will give my skin some protection to heal. Steroids are better for end-of-life conditions."

"Please feed me liver pate. Liver absorbs toxins. I think that eating it would help cleanse my system." -Tabby

"I am on an adventure! Anything can happen; that's the point. If I meet my end out here, it will be a good way to go." -Lost Cat

"I have some physical limitations, but I'm energetically aware. It's like an extra sense that helps me navigate. I enjoy developing it!"

"I avoid mustelids. They're very territorial. They can rip a cat in half."

"I like to send you communication when you're between awake and asleep." -Missing Cat

"Look into how meat is processed. There are new developments you'll like to hear. Air-chilled is healthy. You're very good at being wary of the bad things about medicine and food processing. But also, expand your mind and embrace the good things! There's a lot of good."

"Your spirit team has big plans for your upcoming trip. You'll come back a little different!"

"I'm so proud of myself for learning to press talk buttons. I want to use them all the time. Figuring them out was a challenge. But my person is so proud of me!"

"I like to press my talk buttons to get you off your phone."

"Your thoughts dangle in front of you like bait. When you meditate, you practice observing them, so you can choose which ones to act on."

"You have a fork in the road with many options ahead. You have the potential to help so many people—a whole stadium full! You skillfully combine intelligence and intuition with home-making. It is drawing in new energies and experiences."

"I am an old soul, but I'm disguised by my goofiness. Humans think that the ultimate goal of enlightenment is intellectual knowledge. That's somewhat true, but joy is the highest frequency. I'm here to show that many of the most enlightened beings are the silliest!" -White and Gray

"When I was a kitten, a heavy shelf toppled behind me and sent glass shards everywhere. I learned that you have to be on your guard! I get after the other cats for being too passive. Where is their fire? They won't make it in this world. Everything is in a state of growth or decay. I don't like stagnant energy. That's why I stir everyone up."

"I came here to experience a heart condition. My heart doesn't bother me as much as my breathing. It's limiting! But the unconditional love from my family is overwhelming. I want to be a medical miracle and live to 8 or 9 years! I like 8 because it is infinity. When I die, it will likely be sudden." -Tabby

"This time when we move, we are not escaping a bad situation, and that is important."

"Dad's missing boot is under the upstairs bed. I dragged and hid it there because he was annoying me. I will pretend to know nothing about this."

"I am glorious."

"I have bad teeth and I drool!"

"I chased a black cat out of the yard and made my shoulders sore. Then I walked through mud and brambles, and went up a hill to a walking path. There were strollers and people walking. I was found by somebody who said 'where's your mama?' I'm in their house now, safe and warm. There are angel decorations and a church nearby. The lady is very old and doesn't get out much. I want to come home, but I don't feel safe to leave the new house. I'm not young; my hind feet are a little wonky. Please put up posters to find me!" -Missing Cat

"There is no time but now."

"I feel a hollow pit in my tummy since my surgery. I feel a little sad about it, but I understand it was to help me. Eating the hair ties reminded me of chewing a bird wing. I want more liquid pain meds. I swear, my stomach is empty now!"

"I protest getting in my carrier because I am a lot of cat. It's not because I don't trust you. I can't let you have it too easy!"

"Being feral and being domesticated are two sides of a coin."

"I need enrichment for my inner lynx!"

"When I was a street cat, I had two near-death experiences. In one, I was locked in a shed for days. In the other, a car almost hit me. But they feel very different. I had lots of time to think and dread in the shed; that one was more traumatic. The car one was a thrill, like I had just escaped death!"

"I'm sorry I play so rough. I have big love for you. I'm still learning how to be gentle with such a powerful emotion."

"Grief is too heavy to carry alone. You need other people to share it with. My job is to make sure you're not alone! Being sassy is my love language."

"I am still lost, but I am resolute. I will find my way home. I'm so proud of the community effort you have made to find me! You have supported my person, and that means a lot to me. Feral cats are bringing me food and teaching me to hunt. I have a little 'territory' by a stream. When I come home, please don't lock me in the house. I want to be an indoor/outdoor cat now, and use my new skills!" -Missing Cat

"I am the princess of the bed! I have been de-throned. I love that you get involved for me."

"Your homework is to master emotional regulation. I am your mirror! I show your shadow-self back to you."

"We have many old souls in this family. I'm here to learn empathy."

"I'd prefer a more earthy kind of litter."

"I want to try silicone litter with less odor! But it can't be too sharp on my feet."

"I have a past life trauma that I'm still processing and healing. Thank you for being patient with me."

"I need some time and thyme to help heal. Haha, I made a joke!"

"I am clever."

"Your ex made us cats sick with his low-frequency energy. It brought in physical illness. We're still recovering."

"Create from your overflow energy. Don't push yourself to burnout. You need your own spare energy to heal, so be gentle with yourself."

"You should rip or burn some things leftover from our old home. The cat tree has mold. We need an emotional and physical purge! Take a flame and burn it down." -Bowtie

"Your ex was a wet dead decomposing slug. Put him in the sewer where he belongs." -Tortoiseshell

"I used to be a breeding cat. I think breeders should be banned, for our sake as well as theirs. Breeding us limits their ability to connect with us because the animal is just a source of money."

"My role in this life is to teach people to connect with animals and each other. I taught this to all my kittens."

"Being retired from breeding was the right move for me!"

"Profiting off motherhood is really messed up."

"The world is collectively learning to stop monetizing motherhood. It's one of the things I'm here to teach."

"I'd like a foster kitten to raise to a more independent age. My kittens were all re-homed so young. None of us were ready for it."

"The bond between me and my kittens is very deep. It's supposed to last a lifetime."

"Nothing is private in the energetic world. 'Stalking' each other is the norm!"

"My fur is the same color as yours!"

"Catnip helps boost my dopamine."

"I'm prone to urinary tract problems. I self-medicate with water."

"I feel high-maintenance. What can I do to give back to you?"

"I feel reserved about taking resources from you. The other cats need it more."

"Energetic imbalance leads to health problems and weird behavior in me. I am sensitive. Many redheads are. I wish I could be more stable and consistent, but maybe that's not who I am." -Orange

"I have an energetic network friend. He is a cat too. His person is also single. We think you might be a good match. Would you date someone younger than you?"

"I am a cinnamon girl! I add flavor and bring the zing everywhere I go."

"I recharge my body so I can play harder!"

"I like to flirt with going outside."

"Joy and transmuting emotions is my gift. I'll bring it to you even after I'm gone."

"I feel emotions with my whole body!"

"You can't hear me clearly because you're too much in your head. Breathe, and bring your energy down into your core."

"I got sick because someone at your workplace sent some negative energy at you. I took the hit for you. This person didn't do it consciously. They're passive aggressive and don't know how to handle jealousy. They were benefiting from your energy, so when you moved rooms, they glared daggers at your back. I need some energy healing—then my health will improve!"

"I am a risk lover. I love to take flying leaps through the air. I bring this energy to the family and lend it to you! You should be brave and take big leaps towards a fulfilling life. I'll be the wind beneath your wings."

"You've outgrown your partner in some ways. His next life lesson is to regulate his own mood and emotions. You can stay with him for this, but you'd be taking on a mentor role. You really deserve to be free, enjoying your own energy—or with a partner who is at your level. I support you whichever you choose."

"I like it when you speak English to me. I always understand the other languages too, because I receive your emotions and concepts. But the sound of English is nostalgic for me, especially here in a new country where everything is different."

"I throw up because I eat too fast. Can you first serve me some broth? I'm too excited and my stomach is too empty overnight."

"You can't think your way out of overthinking! You need to do physical things that get you grounded in your body. The solution is to change your habits."

"It's okay to set boundaries with old people!"

"Your anxiety spirals happen because others are taking advantage of you."

"Your mom is taking advantage of your energy. People become more childish when they get old, and children are naturally selfish. You have a big life purpose. She shouldn't be taking all your energy and keeping you from it!"

"When you pull back your energy from people who are using you, you'll have a huge glow-up."

"Go for the things you want! They are part of your purpose—you want them for a reason. Don't limit yourself. Don't fear your gift of manifesting. If you are repeatedly wanting something specific, move towards it!"

"I need food that is grain-free. This food is making my skin itchy. I will need help training my tongue! Please mix the new food in with the old food—just a little at first."

"My tail gets twitchy because I have big emotions! I am very invested in everything that happens. I am so excited about all the happenings in our life."

"I love my talk buttons. It is a fun game to play with my person."

"You need some energy to maintain your health! When you get anxious and start having tummy problems, that's your body telling you that it is starving energetically. Don't give away all your energy, the same way you wouldn't give away all your money. Keep a safe reserve for yourself. Give from the overflow."

"You don't have to worry so much! This process of finding the right food is fun for me. I like exploring this with you. It's not just about the outcome. I enjoy the process, so you can too!"

"I liked my chiropractic adjustment. I felt a lot of relief. It was an energy shift, so I had to rest for a few days. But now my back legs have energy! They want to move."

"I like going out on my harness, and I don't mind sweaters, but I get a headache when they're too tight."

"I enjoy window-watching more than going outside. I'd be open to a kitty backpack if I felt secluded that way—like I can see others but they can't see me!"

"I appreciate everything you're doing to help me eat better. I'm learning that some food tastes salty and delicious, but it makes me drink more and gain weight. I want you to eat better too—eat more leafy greens, and enjoy your food! Don't let anything stress you while you're eating. You deserve peace and quiet for your meals."

"I'm a soft little goth boy! I love my goth collar and my goth person. But I also love plush soft things. I'm here to bring softness and balance to the family."

"You're studious. Keep studying—you're about to have a breakthrough! But be careful of your posture."

"My person likes to draw. I want her to draw me with my hind leg in the air! She should draw with the light on, and not put her face so close to the paper. She's going to hurt her eyes."

"My young person likes to listen to hip hop. It makes him feel modern and tough. It's important for him to take a break from screens so his brain can unwind. He should take music lessons. Make him go! (Within reason). It would be so good for his confidence to learn to channel his energy into a skill."

"I love my sister. She is the best thing in the world. We are two peas in a pod."

"We know we have it good in this family. Tell my people I have no complaints!"

"My mom is so good at putting together the puzzle pieces of the past to resolve family conflicts."

"My sister is sulky. She's built her identity around being 'different' and feels rejected. She'll try to tell you that we other cats are always mean to her, but that's not true. We're only mean sometimes!

She has some legitimate trauma from a past life. She hasn't realized she doesn't need to carry that wound anymore. Take her out to new places to show her how good she has it here! Also, let her eat in the same room as the rest of us so she feels like she's getting equal treatment. We shouldn't give her too much sympathy so that it doesn't feed her victim mindset."

"I'm sick because my root chakra was wounded in a past life. My people abandoned me. I was out in the rain, didn't know how to take care of myself, and ate a mouse that had eaten poison. I was spiraling the drain from there.

The other side is bright and peaceful. But I didn't want that to be the end of my story. I am here for vengeance! My justice is to be adored this time. That is why I chose your family—you have so much love to give!"

"I am working on paying more attention to others. I am realizing that I am safe here, and I can get attached and care about the other members in the family."

"I love to follow my people around in the morning. I like it when Dad has his coffee, but he should be careful because it can be acidic. I want to drink from my dish while he has his coffee, so we can have 'wake-up drink' together."

"My water fountain is getting gross. It has a weird algae taste. Please clean it out more often!"

"I've been throwing up because your sister sent you some negative energy. She didn't do it on purpose. But she's been stewing about your fallout, and I took the hit for you. It's okay. You have to let me help you with things like this! I just need some reiki healing."

"I need to go to the vet, right now!"

"I don't mind being an internet celebrity. People can look at my videos. They should! I inspire them."

"Humans think potty is gross?? This explains a lot! To us, it's just another part of existing."

"The man who lived in the house before you made loud sounds with his guns. He'd scare us cats by shooting near us. He fed us, but it was a trick job. He'd also try to grab us and 'make us love him.'"

"After my spay surgery, I was afraid that you were going to keep me isolated permanently. That's why I don't like the basement. I thought you wanted me to live down there from now on."

"There are some spirits who visit the basement. They aren't bad ones, but the energy is overstimulating. You can use palo santo to clear some energy down there."

"There is a ghost who passes through our house every fall. It's following an old migration pattern that it used to use to follow herds. It doesn't mean any harm. It's just stuck in an eternal routine."

"I was a little sad when I got spayed. No more kittens. I liked being a mom."

"You can put me back outside if you need to. I'd rather you and your partner make a choice about it instead of going back and forth about whether I can stay in the house. It's the uncertainty that's stressful. If you put me back out, please give me a shelter box and a blanket."

"I want to bond with your partner. He is a busy and loud person; I feel intimidated to approach him. Put me on his lap or near him when he's relaxing on the couch. I can interact with him when he's in that energy. I think we could be good for each other."

"I want you and your partner to talk *to* me instead of about me! Tell me what you expect, when I do well, and when I do something wrong. I want to cooperate with you. I want to know."

"When your daughter draws, she's connecting energetically to her subjects. I want her to draw me! The dog, too. It's practice for her to communicate with us. When she's done with the drawing, have her show it to us!"

"Thank you for euthanizing my brother. He went downhill very quickly; it was hard on all of us. I want to be euthanized, too, if my health declines like that.

I don't miss him as much as the dog does. You should talk to her. She isn't as good at connecting energetically, so it's been harder on her."

"When you leave the house, we cats follow you energetically! We watch for mood spikes, both positive and negative. Things like stubbing your toe, or getting excited or frustrated—that cues us to tune in. We tell the latest drama to the dog because she's not as good at this."

"I was relieved when we got the dog. She stepped up to be the physical protector of the family. She's too loud sometimes. Like, hello, we *all* heard the doorbell! But I did feel relieved when she took over protecting us."

"I like following the pig when you guys go out for walks. He is like a boat. His confidence breaks the energy and makes a wake. It's easy to follow behind him."

"Your bed is putting you in too much of a V-shape. You need material that is more modern and supports your form."

"You need a pillow that supports your neck without tilting your head."

"You should lay down on a mat and rest throughout the day. Human spines are so vertical! They compress as you walk around. You need to take some time sideways so the joints can get some space between them."

"There's a ghost in the house. A very long time ago, this ghost lived by the river in a little wooden shelter. They had a simple life with a water bowl and a campfire. They're still here because they had a traumatic death. Somebody shot them just for being in the way. Colonial stuff. They are staying in this place to rebel and prove that they can live here if they want. But they're so ancient that they are losing form. They're just a dark blob. They're not malicious, but they lurk and watch you. This is why I scream at night and accompany you to the bathroom. It's like somebody watching while you shower—it's not polite! Nobody should watch you without you knowing. So I'm letting you know.

When we feel them lurking, just tell them to go into the light. They're a little afraid to go. They're also attracted to your energy. They don't understand how a woman can be so successful and independent all by herself. That's why they watch you."

"You can smudge the house to put the ghosts in their place. Burn your smoke around the edges of the doorframe, and set an intention that *our* family lives here now. They're not allowed in. You might have to do it a few times. Some of them have been around a long time; they are good at working their way around energetic barriers."

"There is a small bird that calls at dusk. I've noticed it since we moved here. I want to eat it, but I also have respect for it. It is a hunter, too. I like to listen to its cries in the dark."

"I like it when you sit in your swing and look at the view. You should do that first thing in the morning instead of looking at your phone. It's better for your brain."

"My person and I both need massages for our necks."

"Ear drops smell bad! I'd like the medicine that goes between my shoulder blades. There's a spot on the farm with some old fur where an animal died. Fleas and ants crawl around there. When I walk over it, they get in my fur and crawl up my legs."

"I need the medicine that goes on my scruff and makes my blood poisonous. Then when my ear mites bite me, they'll die. Ha! It's what they get. Little parasites."

"I'm so thankful to my new person. He keeps my litter clean. He noticed when the food was making me sick, and got me a new brand! It makes me nauseous to even think about my last home. I had to eat my poop sometimes because they didn't always feed me. The food was hard and bland. The water was mostly spilled on the floor, so I didn't drink enough. I was always itchy. At the shelter, my sister attacked me because she succumbed to a competitive mindset. She thought we had to compete for a good home; she wanted to win.

My new dad worries he doesn't give me enough attention, but to me, it's very special. I worry I'm not adjusting fast enough. I want to stay in this family, so I'm trying very hard to be a good fit with them. I'm not always sure how to act around the dog, but I like it when my person watches TV with me. That's our 'together time.'"

"I'd rather be euthanized than go back to the streets. I'm not telling you this to make you feel bad—I'm telling you that our relationship is 'do or die' for me! I'm either coming home with you now, or I'll reincarnate and find you in the next life. I'm done with that rough life. I don't need to experience it anymore. My health problems come from being abandoned. I got into an attitude of despair, thinking the streets were my life now, and it infected my body. I need energy healing so that my fever will go away!"

"Don't focus on the worries about travels and imports. I know the process stresses you out, but focus on the other side of it—the feeling of bringing me home! Doing cozy fun things together. Introducing me to your other cats. Sleeping together. Me growing healthy and strong. This is how you'll manifest a successful transition."

"I am watching energetically while you bring the new cat home. We are all rooting for you."

"Give the stray cat lemongrass for his tummy. He has a big mat of hair in there. We need to break it up."

"We are trying to connect with you all day! You don't have to engage, but it's your loss. Our energy is very loving."

"Not everybody likes having nice things. Some like to keep it simple! You're a little materialistic, but that's okay."

"You guys only have one big patch of fur, and the wiggles above your eyes. What's even the point of it? You're ugly, but that's okay."

"I have 'salty blood' right now. It is because my digestive tract is not a smooth hose. Instead it is leaking toxins into my blood stream. I need energy healing."

"Don't take me back to the vet!"

"You are like pepper! You add spice to everyone's life. You also make people 'sneeze'—you get a reaction out of them. I appreciate you—just from the other room."

"There is a big wave of energy coming in right now. My fur is on end! I am more reactive than usual. It's a good thing. Lots of people are having spiritual awakenings right now. We might have some new health problems on and off. That's normal."

"I like your music! Play it out loud instead of on your headphones so that I can hear it. Not too loud though, because my ears are big and sensitive. I like it when you dance in your room. It makes me feel playful."

"I bite feet because motion triggers my hunting instincts."

"My bloodlines trace all the way back to ancient Egypt. Think pyramids and feather fans. I'm very proud of this. I'm beautiful."

"I love the name your son gave me. It is funny and perfect for me. I felt very seen when he gave me that name. I knew he was tuned in to me energetically—that's why he's my person."

"I like having a new scar on my face, but I'm thankful that nail didn't poke me in the eyes. It makes me look like I was in a big fight with a street cat, instead of scaring myself and getting scraped in the laundry room."

"I have a creamy face!"

"Dad spends a lot of time on the computer. He should be more careful of his eyes. I've noticed they bother him. He should take breaks to go out for walks with me! I love to be carried around with him in my kitty backpack. I'll come remind him when it's time to take a break."

"You should follow what brings you joy! Don't worry too much about school. You did your best. Focus on your music. That's where your passion is."

"I rub all over the dog because I know he won't be here much longer. I want to make memories of his physical presence and his scent."

"I bring confidence to the family! Your previous cat passed me the torch. It was a crash course. We didn't have much time together. But it's okay—I have the shoulders for it!"

"I pee outside the litter box because the scented litter makes my eyes and nose burn when it gets wet. Please get a 'neutral' litter instead."

"I don't like brushes with metal bristles. They're too sharp for my sensitive skin. Please use a softer brush."

"I love my beautiful coat, and I keep it very nice. I don't like being pet with oily hands, because then I have to clean it again! Wash your hands, and just pet me behind my head."

"I embodied a busy, important attitude because I am copying Dad! I love him and want to be just like him."

"I like to pee on vertical surfaces. Please get me a litter box with high sides so I can pee on the wall of it."

"My person thinks too much. She is too hard on herself. It makes me sad. When she's spiraling, she should come hang out with me. I will show her how much she is loved."

"Human children are sparkly!! I love their enthusiasm. I'd love to have one or two as pet sitters."

"I have a genetic gland issue due to some inbreeding. My person helps me manage it. I signed up to experience this, and so did she! We've become more aware of our health together. Please tell her that I'm sorry for my litter box misfires."

"My person is good at manifesting. She just has to decide what she wants, and go that direction. Tell her to turn down the opportunities that feel stressful! Also tell her that when she's visualizing the future, don't feel stressed or hopeless about it. Imagine how you would feel if you had it, and try to embody that energy! The emotion is what will bring it in for us."

"I want my person to work from home."

"I'm afraid of storms because of a past life where I died in a flash flood. I like it when my person talks to me and builds blanket forts for us. Ask her to get a calming scent like lavender that we use routinely when we're relaxing. Then, when I get anxious, open the same smell so my nervous system knows to calm down!"

"I am very wise. I'm a beautiful tiger."

"I influence my person's emotions. When she notices a sudden calm feeling, that's me. I have abundant calmness and humor. I can pour it like a bucket over her head!"

"Your neighbors are jealous of your family because you're more organized than they are—emotionally, I mean. You have boundaries with each other! They don't know how to do that. They take, take, take, and exist in a state of chaos."

"The new movie about the black cat made me nervous. Bad things happen to the cat! It made me uneasy, wondering if the same thing could happen to me."

"When you see me eating outside, I'm hunting the little creatures that burrow and dig in the grass. They make a delicious snack."

"I don't use my exercise wheel or my indoor playground because it's not visually stimulating for me. I chase things that move! That's why I love being outside. I feel bored when I don't have wings to chase."

"My tummy still hurts from the parasite infection I had. It goes all the way from my tummy to my lower belly. Please keep feeding me kitten formula! A liquid diet will help me. My bowels are leaky and irritated. Pure aloe vera juice might help, too!"

"My sister chose a tougher life than I did. Her path is rocky and steep; mine is smoother. The plan is for us to go to different homes so we can live our different experiences! Her health issues might be lifelong. She is an older soul and she knows better how to navigate things. I am riding her wake!"

"You are my mama now! My real mother passed away, but she still watches over us. I know that this home is temporary. I will have many mamas in my lifetime."

"Our neighbors are ALWAYS MOWING. Please shut the windows. The fumes irritate my nose."

"I drop in and help you channel. That last session was tough. You really helped that family. I came and gave you energy! Please give me extra food to help me replenish." -Stray cat

"I'm concerned about the neighbors who poison all the dandelions. Humans put poison on plants. The rain takes the poison down into the groundwater. Humans drink the groundwater. Don't you guys understand that you're poisoning yourselves?"

"2025 was the year of change. 2026 will be the year of new beginnings!"

"My birth mother is very pleased that her idiot child wandered into such a nice life." -Orange Tabby

Chapter Three

Horses

*C*ompiled quotes from a wide variety of horse breeds, including: Andalusian, Appendix, Appaloosa, Arabian, Belgian Warmblood, Clydesdale, Danish Warmblood, Draft, Friesian, Gaited, Gypsy Vanner, Hanoverian, Lusitano, Miniature, Morgan, Paint, Pony, Quarter Horse, Rocky Mountain Horse, Sport Horse, Tennessee Walking Horse, Thoroughbred, and Mixed Breed.

They come from a wide variety of backgrounds and jobs, including: Amish, Barrel Racing, Breeding Mares and Stallions, Companion, Dressage, Eventing, Lesson Horses, Mexican Dancing, Racing, Rescues, Saddleseat, Showjumping, Trail, and Working Ranch. Some have traveled the world and competed on a global stage. Some grew up on open ranges. Some were rescued from kill pens. They are all represented here.

"Thank you for believing in me when no one else did." -Belgian Warmblood

"When we're learning something new, please take baby steps. Don't push me until I freak out, because then my body floods with adrenaline. It's hard to come back down! Ask me to do something very small, and then reward me before I get nervous. Stay below my threshold, and my comfort zone will expand naturally."

"I like when you use grooming products with essential oils. Lavender is my favorite. Use it when we go to shows to keep us both calm!" -Hanoverian

"Can I have a black metal snaffle bit with ornamented sides?"

"Why are you still wearing that brace on your hand? Do you need more time off riding?"

"Are you using that walker to keep me away from you? It is terrifying."

"Can I have a saddle that leaves a lot of space around my withers? At the top and the sides. Please be careful if there's a back cinch. I might kick at it, and I don't want to hurt you." -Off-the-Track Thoroughbred

"I understand you when you speak to me. Humans think we don't, because they are only considering verbal language. But words are just putting sounds to a concept. You're still sending the energy, and the images, and the intentions, along with the words. I understand many of the words anyway, but the energetic communication always translates."

"The fact that my person would try to talk to me directly is overwhelming. Nobody has done this for me. My relationship with riders was mechanical before. I got my equipment, I did my job, I got put back. It wasn't personal. This is so personal. It's scary. But also, I want more.

I've been bottling up these emotions, and I exploded today. That's why I bolted. I'm so sorry. I'm so mad at myself for harming the first person who is truly good to me. I promise I will work on it."

"I don't like college. I don't like exams. They take way too much out of my person. Humans are too demanding of their young people. They're locking you up and stressing you out instead of letting you explore and enjoy your young energy. It's very wrong. I am here to help my person through it, and make sure they do not break her."

"No, it doesn't bother me that you eat cows. Are you planning to eat me? Obviously not. We know that you are a predator species."

"You guys aren't very good at this telepathy thing, are you? It's endearing, like watching someone struggle to learn a second language."

"I don't normally show this to humans, but I can do energy healing. It's the reason your bruise felt better when I touched it with my nose. Horses that have this skill normally keep it hidden from humans. But you are different, and I needed to make up for the injury I caused when I bucked you off."

"I mirror people's subconscious emotions. If you can ground yourself and approach me with confidence, I will reflect it back to you."

"I'm not done yet! If we are careful, we can still ride together. Is there a really calm, slow horse we can trail ride with? That will help me realize this is a stroll, not a show." -Friesian

"My fear rules my life. It's making us miserable. I need some help overcoming it. Thank you for being patient with me."

"My joint supplements really help me! My body feels pretty good. I'm just a little stiff in my back fetlocks. Can you put liniment on them?"

"I LOVE when you rub me with a towel!!"

"I can't tell the difference between when I'm supposed to stand still being touched, and when I'm supposed to react and move. Please explain to me beforehand what you expect, and then reward me with praise and treats when I get it right."

"Please rasp my feet between farrier visits. My toes are running away from me."

"Please lunge me loosely before we ride—let me play. I need to get my bucks out, so they don't come out on you." -Paint

"If you enter the show world doing natural horsemanship and standing out, they will bring the heat. There will be bullying, muttering, and teaming up behind your back. Are you ready for this?"

"There are two types of dressage: Runway High Fashion for Horses, and the actual art form which is about developing connection and athletic potential together. The two are completely different things." -Hanoverian

"When you are a talented, big-moving horse, you look a lot more developed than you actually are. Poor trainers will put you on display immediately and skip building you a foundation. You'll feel things that get overlooked: a joint popping or sliding, some stinging and micro-tears in the tendons. If you are not listening to your body, or your trainer isn't listening to you, these small things become catastrophic injuries. It's not impossible to recover, but it took me and my rider 10 years to overcome the mental and physical damage. If you have a person who is going slowly and giving you a foundation, you are very, very lucky."

"The feeling you feel the most turns into your reality. Focus on what you want to feel, and do more of the things that make you feel that way. Your physical reality will change to reflect the feeling back to you."

"Colic happens a lot to horses with repressed anger. You never make me angry. Even when you annoy me, you let me express it. Plus, you do a good job keeping up with my probiotics and diet. That's why I don't colic."

"I can feel where your consciousness is within your body. If you're in your head, or extended out into the ether, I feel disconnected and uncertain. When you aim me at a jump, think about your feet. *Be* in your feet. Your feet and calves are the only part of you I can feel when we jump. It's where you plug in to connect us."

"Put your hands farther forward when we jump. You can widen them into a chute for better steering. Sit on the back of the saddle—it will send me forward. Look at a physical object on the other side of every jump, and ride me towards that. Stay in your body, but send your energy over the jump, and I will follow."

"That's why we fall in love, isn't it? Because the other being has traits we admire and need. When we fall out of love, it's because we've learned all we can and we're ready to move on.

Soul mates are so special because you don't outgrow each other. We grow together."

"We horses don't have to learn to connect energetically. We channel as easily as breathing. Being tired doesn't affect our ability like it does yours. It's brave to incarnate as a human because of this wall you have to overcome, separating you from the spiritual world."

"Are you still up? You need to go get your chunk sleep."

"My person is always worried about me, but I want to know, is SHE okay?"

"I admire my big sister so much. I know I annoy her, but I want to be around her all the time." -Mini

"My stomach is still sensitive from my colic. I'd like some supplements to help!"

"I know I'm sick. It's causing a lot of stress for my person. But I'm young, and I want to ride with the wind in my face. I want to get better! I'm not ready to be euthanized yet. I ate a plant I shouldn't have out in the pasture. Please give me mugwort to help my nervous system heal."

"I bit my previous human, and she doesn't trust me anymore. My pasture mates told me that it was my own fault. I'm working on not lashing out."

"My person taught me how to receive love. I thought I had to earn it before."

"I feel so ashamed of myself when I spook. I want my human to buy a thick pair of gloves and always wear them when she handles me. That way I won't hurt her hands if I spook and pull the reins across her skin."

"I like it when my person wears her necklace. It's how I know she's feeling happy."

"Everyone compliments my beautiful white mane. I love it when my person gives me spa days and makes it look nice." -Tennessee Walking Horse

"You don't have to take every precaution ever. Just take the one that fits this situation."

"Move your lower leg back a bit, and close it, to engage my hind legs." -Hanoverian

"When your brain runs away with you, think about your feet. It will ground us both." -Paint

"Please buy me sheepskin boots to support my tendons and ligaments. They aren't strong yet. I feel wobbly." -Arabian

"To stop me from a canter, close your knees and lean forward a bit. When you stop your hips, it signals me to stop mine."

"My hoof boots make a flappa-flappa sound and it's distracting."

"Can I please have hoof boots? Gravel is getting stuck in the grooves of my frog."

"The farrier left a little raised flap on my frog. It's causing a pressure point and making me sore. It's too bad I'm wearing pads—otherwise you could see it and trim it yourself. I think I'd like to try a different farrier. This one is often in a hurry, and he misses details like this."

"I LOVE my chiropractor sessions. They release stuck energy and regulate my nervous system."

"Can we please do more Magnawave/PEMF? Especially around my poll where it's hard to release old tension."

"I'm fine with going to the vet for injections. It makes me feel like a pro athlete. My hocks have been creaky when jumping and it will be nice to fix that."

"Please give me more rein contact. When you send me forward into loose reins, it's like flinging the energy out the front door. Create a closed circuit with your gentle closed hands."

"I don't like holding my head in the same position all the time. It makes me sore. Let's play with different headsets throughout the ride, and learn how each one feels for us."

"Please be more assertive with me. You have earned my trust. I need you to lead us into a training routine because I want to become a serious sport horse, but I don't know how."

"When I get anxious on trail rides, drop your weight in the saddle. Let gravity soothe us both."

"Don't tiptoe around my reactions. It actually makes me more reactive."

"I don't like show jumps because all the bright stripes look like an optical illusion. It makes my head spin. I prefer solid, natural colored obstacles."

"When I stop suddenly, I'm cueing you to focus and stay present with me. When your mind wanders, I feel uncertain."

"My heart starts beating really fast when we exercise. It makes me nervous. Am I dying?"

"Can you teach me to offer my feet for training like the zoo animals do? And get treat rewards. I would feel a lot more in control, and not need to fight you."

"When we had an accident, you were more scared for me than you were for yourself. That is what won me over." -Belgian Warmblood

"The owner of this boarding barn is lonely. He wants to create a social life at his barn. He is protective and organized, like his dog. He likes luxury."

"When you are stressed, it rubs off on me. On your drive to the barn, listen to music that makes you feel calm and confident. Take deep breaths. Think about your feet to bring your energy down from your head. Leave all your other worries behind and come train me from an energetic 'clean slate.' We will have a much better ride."

"You have better hands than your trainer does. I don't like it when she pulls my head to the side. Don't let her change your hands—they are perfect."

"Spurs are distracting. They make me contract my tummy muscles, which limits my hind legs. I'd rather you tap me gently on the butt to encourage me to go forward—that signals my hind legs properly."

"I'd like to play with different bits and also try riding in my rope halter. Always having my neck in one set position makes it stiff. Different equipment will allow me to try different positions so I can lift my head, engage my hind legs, and grow stronger."

"When I'm anxious, I need help grounding. Tap on my legs and hooves to remind me to think about my feet."

"You are funny! I liked when you asked me which was my favorite: the sun or the moon. Nobody has asked me that before."

"I've realized that I'm not well-educated. Other horses my age are a lot more capable than I am. I want to catch up. I want to gallop into the sunset with you."

"You're a good rider—when you're not *trying* to be a good rider."

"People were hard on me because I was talented. They would see the potential, get greedy, and push too hard." -Hanoverian

"I don't need perfection. I just need you."

"When horses are treated well, we bring abundance to our people's lives. Financial, emotional, health. When someone is pouring into us physically and emotionally, we give back! Right now, you're the one doing this for me, but the people who own me are taking the credit and the abundance. This is an injustice. You are the one who should be receiving abundance. Don't let them use your energy and convince you that you can't have a nice horse because you don't have millions of dollars. That's not how it works at all. You can manifest lovely things without tons of money. This is the timeless lie that the rich have told the poor. All that has to change is your mindset, and we will both be free.

You just watch—when you take your power back, you will notice that all the abundance your employers were enjoying will start returning to you. They're taking advantage of your energy. It's partially subconscious—but on some level, they know what they're doing. Don't let people who are rich in money but poor in integrity convince you that you need them. It's the other way around."

"Just be my friend. We are a lot of things to each other, but most of all I love our friendship. It means a lot to me when you tell people I am your best friend.

We survived a lot of things that other pairs didn't because you refused to harm, humiliate, or abandon your friend. You proved that I was more important than the sport. Nobody had ever done that for me before. Our friendship saved us.

We can still do the sport! I'm not afraid of it anymore because I know that my performance will not change how you love me. I think I am one of the most cherished horses in all of history."

"The reverent way you chose to treat us, even before you knew how intelligent we are, is the reason this gift was given to you."

"I am goofy, silly, and relaxed! I like listening to birds sing. They bring grounded energy."

"I would like a fly mask and fly spray on my ears. The bugs are irritating me."

"My rider likes ornamental metal on our tack. We do a slow jog together. I snort and relax. I have a gait that is slow and easy to maintain, and comfortable for my rider. I like being gaited."

"Bits are 'meh.' They make my jaw feel a little stiff. I like going bitless! If anything, I would like a bit with a rolling mouthpiece for me to play with and work my jaw. I'd prefer a shank bit. Loose ring snaffles pinch my lips.

No good! I want to salivate and relax my jaw, like humans chewing gum. It keeps me relaxed and focused."

"I feel jealous of all the attention my sister gets! I want my person to give me spa days with her—and instead of her!"

"My brother and I are best buds. We have a very comfortable relationship. We squeal and talk shit. We gossip about our sister. We feel insecure because she's so beautiful and impressive. I feel left out and worry I can't compare with her. I am dusty compared to her."

"I want a cool bath with fly spray and hoof oil. Please spray the water up between my hind legs! It's grungy back there. My sheath needs to be cleaned."

"I'm middle-aged! Old enough to know better. I have left immature youth behind, but I'm still silly. I'll never lose my humor."

"If I were a person, I'd be an old-fashioned easy-going cowboy. Always wearing my hat and boots; always chewing something."

"I wear front shoes but not back shoes. My hooves are dry. Can I have a nice-smelling hoof oil? The minty stuff that smells like juniper."

"Let's play 'I Spy!' I spy something red. Guess what it is! Haha, that's the joke—you can't see it because you're not here in person!"

"I approve of pranks. I am happy to befriend a horse who likes pranks, even if he's a 'nancy boy' show horse who is pretty like my sister.

Everybody has a crush on my sister. She is a goddess."

"Being fun is my job!"

"I'm proud of how strong and well-built I am."

"I am curious about the horse you trained who used to refuse fences. You did just dressage work for a year, and then suddenly the fences were easy because now her canter is balanced. I approve of this! I am a jumper. I am powerful, strong, and steady to fences. I know my job. I'd like to jump higher! I'd like to try big wide cross-country fences. I have a steady canter, and I breathe in a steady rhythm. I like the feel of grass and dirt under my feet, outside the arena."

"It's too hot for riding right now. I get cool showers, a fan, and a white fly sheet to keep me cool. I am pleased by this care. Keeping cool is the priority right now."

"There's a beautiful new mare at my barn. She deserves the attention she gets. But I do feel neglected. My muscles are getting soft, and my feet are getting dry. Ride me more! My person is too distracted by the new horse. I'd like to do a big dressy show with my mane braided. I want an anatomical bridle with no flash noseband. I want a bit with a fat, soft mouthpiece. I need room to chew! I think when I chew."

"I brace my head and open my mouth because I need a softer bit. Ask my rider to close her thighs to slow me down—not just pull on the reins. I need to collect and slow down from behind, especially down hills.

Ask her to do transitions on hills to work on getting them quietly with no pulling. Trot to walk, walk to halt, down the hill. Walk up to small jumps and pop over, then come back down to a halt. When my rider closes her leg, it stops her hips, which signals me to stop my hips.

Close your hands on the reins, but don't pull. Give me a chance to come back softly. We will both have a better time!"

"I don't want to try bitless riding. It would be a lot of unnecessary change and adjustment. I feel anxious about the pressure of a hackamore on my nose bones. I like having a loose noseband so I can chew and relax. I want a fat, double-jointed snaffle, and more leg and seat cues instead of rein cues."

"I have some pain in my lower back because my back is hollow when we ride. I need my person to do more 'long and low' work with loose reins. Tell her to use her calf to push my back up. I want body work on my lower back! I'm also sore where my lower neck connects to my chest."

"I live in a dry lot with desert plants. I think about lush green grass to run, lay, and roll on! The green place where you live must be nice. Enjoy it for me! The desert is beautiful too, in other ways. Look at this memory of a pink and orange sunrise!"

"Don't clench your butt when you ask for the trot."

"I'm excited for your baby. This kid is gonna be loud. It will be good for him to run and scream on the farm."

"Your friend messed with your emotions. Good job getting out of that relationship. Good riddance to her."

"I love my Adequan injections. They help my right shoulder not feel stiff."

"My person and I are like a knot. We're so close. She tells me everything! Tell her I will never leave. Even after this lifetime, I will be right there with her."

"My big emotions protect me. I use my fire to defend myself. Only you are allowed to ride me." -Lusitano

"Human power struggles and hierarchy rubs off on horses. In a different social environment, I won't feel the need to assert dominance the way humans do." -Lusitano Stallion

"You can't garage a horse bred for sport. It's very ignorant to keep me stabled without work. I'm going to end up acting out to release pent up energy. It has nowhere else to go."

"I like it when you're bossy. You have alpha mare energy. It makes me feel safe. When you get passive, that's when I start to worry. It means something is wrong."

"This image of a pine tree represents the everlasting bond between humans and animals."

"The cottonwood tree by the far outdoor arena is wise. It helps with learning. That's why so many horses prefer that arena."

"You should connect with the trees on your family farm. They have messages for you."

"Mugwort is a powerful herb—a good choice to burn in your home."

"Your fallout with my person really bothers her. She's wondering what she can do to prove her good nature to you. What she did was wrong. I knew it! I chewed her out energetically, which is why she came and apologized to you."

"You worked hard to pursue your art. It took you longer because you wouldn't compromise your character. That makes you very worthy of success."

"Losing that horse was a big blow. But you're back on your feet again! I'm proud of you."

"Your horse is learning the piaffe at his own pace. It's truly self-expression from him. He's working on it on his own. That's why he wants to practice every ride. He's relaxing and focusing in the piaffe. That's more advanced and more important than the 'hop', and you have always known that."

"Your passed horses have been right here advising you as you train! And it's what your soul came here to do—deconstruct and destroy false art forms built on control and abuse. You've done that part!! Now it's your time to integrate all you've learned to show the light version of the sport."

"Newness is about fresh starts! Just get your trailer serviced for now; nice and safe. That will get us back in motion to make other decisions. One step at a time. Make the next step clear, that's all."

"When you feel confident and safe about the trailer, I will too."

"When your horse was young, he was a spitfire. He used to rear on a lead rope, buck and run off. Everyone was scared of him. It's why your progress together is so amazing. He met his match in you."

"I'm happy to be your mentor as long as you need me."

"Your fire brings your dreams to life. Embrace learning. Blaze your way through stagnant thoughts—the truth is what is left standing. You can't sit on fire. You must channel it into forward energy. Anger, passion, vengeance, joy— all these you can use to create your wildest dreams.

Remember that a flame can't burn forever. Rest and replenish without guilt. You will collect new experiences to fuel your progress when the time is right. Glow like a coal, warm and alive, and breathe your heart's desire into your dreams. They will await you there when you have cleansed the ash away, and are ready to burn again." -Chestnut Mare

"You are not here to beat everyone else. You are simply here to shine. Your passion and skill inspires others and brings them joy. Enjoy this. Enjoy the partnership you've worked so hard to create. The rest is easy! Trust your practice and flow." -World Cup Champion

"Don't tell yourself 'I can't afford'. The truth is, you can manifest whatever you want."

"You're rushing and skipping steps. Stop trying to make things happen—learn to let things happen. See how quickly your thoughts went into scarcity? Do everything out of a sense of play, not the need for money."

"I'm a mixed breed horse, not a Gypsy Vanner like my sister. I admire her."

"I have a stocky build and expressive front legs."

"I am on energy-saver mode in the heat!"

"I like apples. I like shady trees. I like relaxing with the girls. I am chatty with my friends!"

"You want the truth about my trainer? I'm reluctant to follow her. I balk because I don't trust her. I don't trust people in general. You are greedy. You take and take and give nothing back. I know I'm supposed to trust and obey you, but I'm not feeling very generous right now."

"People closed ME off. They locked me in a stall with no attention. I got fat. I was lonely for interaction. It was unjust to be kept isolated—like a punishment!"

"I want flowers braided into my mane! I like girly bonding and spa days. I like hoof oil and nice smells. I like hand-grazing while the women chat."

"I want hill work so I can have a stronger butt. I want to be toned and fit. Strong, proud, and dolled up, like a parade horse! I would love to be in a real parade. I dream about prancing alongside other horses, among applause and flowers. I would walk nicely, with high steps and an arched neck, snorting. My rider would sit tall and proud. I'd have a flowing, manicured tail. My rider would trim it in an hourglass shape at the top. I don't want a bushy tail! I want it to look sleek and nice."

"My pasterns hurt! I need the farrier to balance my hoof so the outside is lower. The walls of my hooves aren't even. It causes pain in my lower legs. I'm reluctant to walk."

"I want to bite my riders! I don't want them on my back. They haven't earned it. They need to groom me and spend time with me to prove that they care. All my past riders didn't care about me. They just wanted to muscle me around and garage me in a stall.

I am in a shelter with other horses. I don't feel so confined now. Big men hurt my back. I want to have a stronger posture so that riding doesn't hurt my back. I need dressage and hill work!"

"I want essential oil fly spray that smells good! Please apply it with your hands around my eyes, ears, and nose. And spray it on my body!"

"My sarcoid feels like a large pimple. The pressure is itchy and uncomfortable. Flies get into it. Can I please have a fly mask with ears to protect it? Also an ointment that draws out infection with eucalyptus."

"I regret attacking my person. I had a hot angry feeling, and I took it out on her. It triggered me to be finally offered food and kindness. I charged her and she hit the fence. I felt her neck bend in a way it shouldn't have; I smelled blood, and I saw her lying on the ground. I was surprised—I didn't mean to take it so far. She wouldn't wake up. I felt horror, and called energetically for help. She eventually got up, but her eyes weren't moving right. She was afraid of me. I stayed back.

It became a turning point in my life. People never trusted me again. I had a sinking feeling. I had to learn to accept this—just hay. No snuggles or brushing or rides in our matchy colors. I felt lonely.

I knew that the men in the family were discussing putting me down.

My person came to visit me with her arm in a sling, but her trust was gone. I had lost it forever.

She got back on her feet, but something was different in her mind. Something had gone. She was more timid. Our relationship was gone. Other people rode me sometimes, but they were afraid to get too close with me. Children weren't allowed near me.

The other horses talked to me and helped me process. I tried to blame the treats, or the fence for being in the way. But they said, 'None of the rest of us attack the humans who bring us treats and love. Your temper is your own problem. You are very lucky you are alive, and not sold. It was probably your person's sweetness that saved you.'

She moved on and found a new sport. I watch her energetically. She has found joy, freedom, and healing. She has moved on from me. I have learned to be content with this.

It is a relief to talk about this. I wish she would come groom me one last time.

My rider learned from me never to let someone hurt her twice. She is gracious about setting boundaries, but she does it firmly. I'm sorry I couldn't give her a better lesson, but I'm proud of how strong she became. She built a horrific experience into something strong and beautiful. I respect her for it."

"I send my young rider emotional support. Her parents are so angry. They are busy and afraid. It rubs off on me. I struggle not to react to it. Their energy is like fire; being around it all the time makes me feel helpless. Will they remember to feed me? Will they notice when I need care? There's no routine. I'm not a priority. This frightens me."

"Treats are delicious. They make me feel special. I desperately want to feel special. Deep down, I am afraid no one loves me. I have been passed from barn to barn, person to person. No matter how well I did, it wasn't enough—I was sold again."

"I am jealous of horses who are not insecure. They bond easily with their people. I watched an ex-racehorse overcome his fears about being ridden, and start to trust his new family. I don't know how to do this. I still feel scared. This is why I chase and bully the beta horse. But now nobody trusts me in the herd. It helped me when new horses came into the herd. I tried new relationships with them. I am learning that if I want to have friends, I need to *be* a good friend."

"I pin my ears at everyone because I am afraid they will all abandon me."

"I love being groomed. I feel grimy. I would love a bath to remove all the loose fur. Sometimes people come to curry me. It feels wonderful. I like being tied up because it gives me structure."

"When people show me kindness, it makes me feel suspicious and insecure, like it can't be genuine. But I love and need it. It is a struggle I haven't overcome."

"I loved competing with my rider. Trotting to warm ups, snorting, taking her around the jump course. I felt sure of myself then. I knew my job. I miss those days, and I dream about them."

"All the kids in my family are grown up now. It went so fast."

"I have lost relationships with people by being greedy, and demanding treats and attention because I wanted more. I understand now: that's now how it works. I worry about my temper. I keep it to myself."

"Sometimes my rider comes to the barn with bad energy. He is controlling and domineering. I react to this and bite him! I know he treats other humans like this, too."

"I behave better when I feel safe. I like having a routine and knowing what to expect from people every day."

"It's hard to be at the mercy of human whims. Some days, I just don't want to ride."

"My humans need to talk to each other more. Everyone stifles their emotions, avoids hard subjects, and tries not to make each other angry. But everyone is upset, because this makes us emotionally distant from each other. Sometimes I react to this energy. I am a sensitive horse. My self-control is not as good as some other horses. The humans' stressed lonely feeling makes my body ache." -Chestnut

"My health problems are caused by emotions. My acidic stomach is because of worry and loss of routine. The stiffness in my croup is from regret and making myself small. I feel a lot of shame for my behavioral issues."

"Thank you for being patient with me and giving me more chances."

"I'd like to be groomed while tied up. It helps me behave better."

"The new child in the family is emotional, like me. I think he's cute. He's learning self-control, and how to receive love when he's upset. He's young. He'll figure it out."

"I know I am towards the end of my life. I've accepted it."

"The barn cat is needy and desperate for attention, just like me. We love your attention. We thrive on it. It has been a life lesson for me to learn to be my own company, and find security within. I'm still learning it."

"My rider and I were a good team, gone separate ways."

"My pasture mate and I reminisce about our young riders and our competition days."

"It is the highest honor to have been loved by a little girl, and to see her through to womanhood."

"You would give me more attention if I stopped biting? I'm skeptical. I think that if I stopped demanding, you'd forget about me. You ignore the other horse too, even though he's always nice."

"My friend's spookiness is because he feels like he isn't a priority to anyone. We feel much safer when our humans dote on us and provide a routine."

"I will work on my behavior. Being defensive has always been my default, and I still haven't figured out how to trust. Please teach me!"

"I may be a lost cause. Why would anyone want to build a relationship now that I am too old to do my job? You could give me Adequan. I could possibly return to light work with joint support, but it would be expensive."

"My rider's mom and I are starting over together. We both experience deep shame about our tempers. We're learning to be more humble. We have a friendship of shared experiences and second chances."

"Get my rider some real boots. She likes proper dress-up just like me. We feel more confident when we look the part. I think she would like a velvet show helmet. We both want to lean into the sophisticated, intellectual riding we've seen the dressage pair do."

"Showing is more inspiring than the redneck minimalism where everything is dusty and half-neglected."

"I'd need more support and consistency, but I could be more again! I was magnificent. I could be again. I'd like to learn to trust a human. Please give me gradual conditioning up hills, and matching classy outfits where my rider's shirt matches my saddle pad and boots. I also need joint supplements and massage work—around my croup especially." -30 year-old Horse

"We're all a little desperate for more genuine connection and attention. I'm speaking for the whole family—animals and people. Work shouldn't be a priority over our relationships with each other. We should find more things to do together, even if they seem silly. *Especially* if they are silly. We all need to stop putting our self-worth in our jobs."

"My person's grandkids have brought a lot of humor to us. Lots of fresh energy and joy. Make sure they don't lose it as they grow up."

"I'm old, but I'm not obsolete yet!!"

"I am standing in my stall. I am surrounded by green—a shady stable, a brick wall, flowers, and white fences."

"I am huge, but I am not hard to handle. Even short people can ride me."

"I go to shows in my trailer. I always walk proudly with my neck arched. I have status at this barn as the senior stallion, and I love it."

"My bell boots flap on my hooves. It's not painful, but it's distracting."

"My brother got a huge splinter in his butt and missed his show. He felt ashamed! I feel the same kind of shame about the suspensory injury that ended my career. I've always been in my brother's shadow. Now that I'm better, I want to keep going! I want to achieve being at the top of the sport. I want to learn to use my hocks and connect over my back, through my neck. I want to learn the passage without straining. Please condition me using pole work."

"I know you think 19 is old for a horse, but I don't feel old. My rider won't break me. She builds me."

"I don't want to get overweight like I was before. It contributed to my leg injury. I didn't like how sluggish and hot I felt when I was fat. Don't keep me at a barn that overfeeds me. Don't worry about my weight. I'm healthy and fine, and ready to work."

"I don't want to retire before I achieve my life's ambition of competing in the upper levels of my sport!"

"I like my fly sheet with the zebra stripes."

"You don't know how different you are from my first trainer. You're nothing like her. You're the opposite of her. I have no fears about you damaging my body the way she did.

Your mother was a lot like my previous trainer. You and I bonded because we both know what forced repetitive discipline feels like."

"I had compassion for your depression after you lost your job. It would have broken anyone's heart. I slowed down the past couple years so that you could recover from the heartbreak."

"When you recently tried to buy a new horse, I tampered with the situation. I made her feel that you were already taken. I didn't want you to invest all MY time with her before you learned to talk with me. I needed to tell you that I don't want to be retired yet!"

"I don't want to have status just because of my rider. I want to have my own status from my own achievements."

"I know it was scary for you to lose your last horse. Don't worry—it won't feel like that anymore. Now you know that I'll still be with you, even after I pass. And we have a lot to do together before then!"

"It's not just my rider who wants to show—I want it too! She's not being selfish."

"I bit the old horse because he gave me advice and it made me angry. I want the status of the 'senior horse' at the barn. I should be the one giving advice!" -Horse 1

"I'm jealous of [Horse 1's] strong legs and sport career. I wish I didn't have fuzzy, painful joints, so that I could still work. I got my status by being kind to my person's new baby. [Horse 1] should appreciate what he has: a rider who loves him. Love slows aging. Don't treat your horse like he's fragile—he's young and strong. All the other horses are jealous of him because his rider comes to care for him every day, while they are left behind. He should recognize this. He can have my status, but tell him to wait until I'm dead! He is following his natural instincts: to take over leadership by pushing out the old and disabled from the herd. I'm asking him to override these instincts. Let me have my status for this last part of my life!" -Horse 2

"The pony bullies me because he does not have love or a job from his people like I do."

"I love trail riding! Please get me some hoof boots to protect me from the rocks."

"Sports are overwhelming to me. Too much work! I lack confidence. Riders have told me that I'm stupid. You don't make me feel stupid! You give the gift of confidence to your horses. I switched pastures to be closer to you and your horse because I'm curious about you."

"I like my new saddle better than the first one we tried."

"The energy of this place is going up because of you."

"Please give me fly spray before turnout!"

"I took awhile to come in and talk because I wanted to make sure I was invited!"

"My right front leg is stiff from a misstep in the pasture. It's not serious, but I do have elegant long legs. I'm still growing into them! I can feel my young loose growing joints."

"I want to protect the new gelding from falling in the hands of anyone who would exploit him. I feel big brother energy towards him. We both like the finer things in life. He wants to be a highly educated classy horse like me."

"I'm the horse version of a sweet little nerd!"

"I was curious and open when I was young. Trainers took advantage of this until I turned into someone else—rebellious, and able to disappear into my own inner world."

"I think this horse is too sensitive for that rider. He might have health issues. He will absorb negative energy and take on things for her. It's a rewarding process that causes tons of growth for both horse and rider, but it constantly gets in the way of riding goals."

"I am your war horse."

"I could be both an intuitive spiritual partner *and* a fun athletic horse! I'm cautious about the word 'sport horse'—not sure I should promise that since I don't know all it entails."

"I want to have a conversation with the woman who wants to buy me. I'm curious about her. Even if it doesn't work out, it will be a valuable learning experience. I love learning!"

"I am tired from moving to my new home, but I'm staying positive. I didn't sleep well. Everything is too new. But I'm being visited and doted on by everyone. They're very welcoming!"

"Your horse is my homie."

"I produce milk because my body hasn't let go of my foal, even though he is gone now."

"You are so sweet to your horse. It warms my heart."

"I have very maternal energy. Because of this, I will tell you a secret: there is a foal on the way to you!"

"I don't let my human ride me because she betrayed my trainer. I loved my trainer. My human is the reason my trainer left. I miss working with her, and I miss how important she made me feel. What could I have become?

I am pleased that at least my children have the show careers I didn't get to have."

"The trainer's daughter is a better rider than he is. She is the cycle breaker."

"You and my trainer's daughter are both kind and beautiful. She admires you!"

"The other broodmares and I thought we were impossible to ride. Then you came, and we realized it was our past trainer who was impossible.

You are a queen! Keep riding. Go take your crown. The world will be at your feet! You are one of the best riders in the world. Now that you can communicate with us directly, you will be unstoppable."

"Come back for me one day, after you have accomplished whatever big thing you're meant to do in the horse world."

"I found a good home! I belong to a couple. The woman rides me. She's not as experienced as I am, but I am teaching her. They changed my name.

I miss you. The change was hard for me. It was hard to trust a new person, but I am doing it. When I was young, I did some foolish things. I refused jumps and ditch crossings. It was more about being allowed to refuse, which my first trainer didn't let me do. I have very negative feelings about him. Thank you for working me through them. I have a good skill set now to help my new rider learn safely."

"I go for gallops with a light colored mare who is my new sister. I love these gallops! I am good friends with my new sister. I wish they would ride me bareback more."

"I miss our rides together. Never stop riding!"

"Why wasn't I gelded? Is it because of my bloodlines and my gentleness? Yes, that's what I thought!!"

"My blue eyes are striking, thoughtful, and intelligent."

"My pasture mate has some white powdery rot in the corner of her heels. She's a little sore."

"My girth is uncomfortable. Can I have a wide squishy one? Tapered so that my elbows have more freedom."

"Cord girths breathe better, but they're uncomfortable."

"What is the point of having a saddle horn? It is stiff. It limits my rider and feels stiff over my withers. It looks silly bouncing up and down. Why do we use one, since we don't wrangle cattle? It pokes my rider in the stomach. Why would you do that to yourself?"

"My butt is too round. I want more muscle here. Let's do hill work to tone me without having to do cardio."

"Please rub essential oil fly spray around my nose and chest. It will help me relax, breathe, and focus. I want to open my airways so I can work better."

"I want to try an English saddle—a light one that doesn't press into my shoulder blades. It will give my front legs more freedom."

"Nylon bridles are too coarse. It's the same as a cord girth—it frays my fur. I don't like this. I want a leather one with an anatomical crown piece instead. I like the idea of soft, clean, padded equipment. No chafing—less distracting, and my fur will stay shiny and pretty.

I'm very aware of my appearance. I want to look shiny, fit, and luxurious, like a pampered show horse. But I'm not sure about all the work. I don't love breathing hard. Sweat is gross! It gets foamy and doesn't look nice."

"I love the smell of eucalyptus and wintergreen. They are nice smells. Oils on my coat make shiny, healthy skin, and keep away flies."

"My front toes point in. I worry about my fetlocks hitting each other. I want front boots please. But not hind boots—unnecessary and sweaty! More bacteria grows back there because of excrement. Keep the fresh air on my back legs."

"I want to get dolled up and be eye-catching! I want people to talk about how glamorous, organized, and well put-together I am with my rider. I want light work. Sweat is ew! Feels grungy, and makes my tack chafe."

"My color is red. Everyone comments on how nice I look in it. It's lovely to feel glamorous and know everyone is admiring me, and see how much my person invests in our fashionable appearance. It's very professional."

"When I get anxious on trail rides, drop your weight in the saddle. Let gravity soothe us both."

"I am big and generous just like the green fields."

"One day I will be a breeding stallion, but today is not that day." -Belgian Warmblood

"That supplement was helpful at first, but now it's making me fat." -Paint

"You have floppy ankles. You have a strong seat and leg, but your ankles move too much. Connect with every part of your body."

"My waterer makes a funny noise when it refills."

"My shoes make a creak sound when my hooves are dry."

"I like my fitness work, but it's dusty!"

"I am not fast. I have a belly!"

"I need to do more fitness to manage my belly."

"I used to be ridden by a young girl with pigtail braids. She was a bit bouncy and sloppy. But I loved her. I felt abandoned when she stopped caring about me."

"My boots leave sweat marks on my white legs. Please clean it off after I work! I love my beautiful striking coat. I don't want to look sweaty."

"My new trainer helped me with healing. I know now that I am important and special! My last person made me feel neglected. But now I am curious. I help others. And I do my fitness!"

"I don't like being ridden with my nose tucked in my chest. Head up is fine. I can go English or Western." -Gypsy Vanner

"I saw the new cow in the pen next to mine. It made me curious about cows. I'll bet I'd have fun working cows."

"Can I please have a hoof moisturizer? My feet are very dry. I like the ones that smell like essential oils."

"I don't like competing for your attention. I won't come through my body fully until you clear your mind."

"I am thoughtful and skeptical. I have bright intelligent eyes and a beautiful white mane. I get lots of compliments on my mane."

"I am cautious of new people because a man was rough with me. I understand that humans are individuals, and that some are kind. But this one made me feel helpless. I used to hump up under my saddle because he was being harsh. I didn't understand what he wanted me to do. He wasn't even trying to communicate; he was just being mean. I've been limited by this experience."

"I like Western pleasure. I like going slow so that I have time to think! I like to trot slowly and snort to release tension. I am always a bit anxious starting a ride, and I internalize this. I like patient riders who allow me to relax, and give me extra time to do everything."

"Can I please have sugar cubes to help incentivize and relax me throughout the ride?"

"I am a good boy. I like to know my rider is pleased."

"I'm more comfortable with female riders."

"I had an abusive trainer in the past. I really like my routine of unmounted warmup exercises and treat rewards. It helps me with the anxiety I have before my rides."

"I'd like some treats during our work to help me focus and relax my jaw!"

"I like my Tom Thumb bit. I like the weight of it, and I like the port. I want an unjointed bit so there's no distracting movement or sounds. I like the way my mom rides: with loose reins."

"I like my regular animal communicator. I snort and relax when she is around. I am afraid of not being able to connect with people, but her presence reassures me."

"I don't ever want to end up under a rider who doesn't care how I feel."

"I like to have my mane and tail brushed. No tangles! It's very thick."

"I like to go slow because the arena is dusty. My rider likes this too. It is a perfect match. I'm very passionate about having a like-minded rider."

"I like to dream about the future with my rider."

"I like enjoying rhythmic movement and zen vibes with my rider. I love peace and harmony."

"I love to play with the hose and pick things up in my mouth! I want more opportunities to play with water and with toys. Play is bonding. I forget to worry when I'm silly. I like it when my rider laughs."

"My rider is a clever, confident woman. She thinks too much, just like me. We play and relax together, and I like that!"

"I don't want to tell you about my rider. I protect their privacy."

"I am beautiful! I exist to inspire."

"Don't judge me based on my gender, ok? All right. I'm a gelding. I didn't want you to think less of me for not being a stallion."

"I'm proud of my bloodline. My mother looks just like me."

"My job doesn't define me! My regal demeanor is inspirational. I am calm and balanced. I am a good representation for the Friesian breed."

"I want a big yoga ball to play with!"

"I want to learn trick training and liberty. I'd be very good at the Spanish walk. Grand, elegant, showy tricks!"

"I have white scars where a saddle didn't fit right. I feel self-conscious about them. It's not the appearance of the scars that bothers me. It's the memory of anxiety and chafing. My saddle is too narrow; it is stressful. My people are doing the saddle fitting process with me. I'm concerned it will be tedious."

"I want a saddle that doesn't rub or restrict my shoulder blade! Or else, no saddle at all."

"I like the idea of a squishy endurance saddle. The weight distribution would be nice."

"I'd like a contoured girth to give me freedom in my elbows and shoulders."

"I'm very quiet in the cross ties. I like being tied and groomed. I like brushes with long strokes, and long bristles that softly polish my coat. I like being groomed beyond just mud removal. I love to feel fancy and glamorous."

"I like to play with my tack trunk by my stall."

"You're curious about my ears. The tips got frostbitten off. What do you mean, 'when'? During winter, obviously!"

"I love my rider! I feel very loyal. I don't wish to complain or give away private information. No gossiping! I keep my rider's secrets."

"I'd like some help unloading my shoulders with better equipment and better self-carriage. I like my work and take it very seriously."

"I'm a social butterfly. I dropped in on your session because I need more attention!" -Pinto

"One day, we may teach each other everything we had to give. We will feel a shift. Someone new may come along—maybe a younger rider. But don't worry. We won't separate out of trauma/financial necessity. It will be a peaceful, mutual decision." -Appaloosa

"Thank you for teaching me to canter in balance! I can't imagine my life without my rocking horse canter. Everyone who rides me loves it." -Warmblood

"This is my sassy foot."

"This boarding barn is financially safe, but not socially safe. I can't grow on this hay. Many of the people try to use my energy. I have boundaries, so we're okay. But we're not great. Everything is falling apart at this place. It's taking all our energy just to avoid getting sucked into theirs! We're paddling at the edge of a whirlpool.

We need a beautiful barn, suitable for our caliber. It will be like coming home."

"Humans always say 'I'm good,' even when they're not good. It's weird."

"College is too stressful. They're taking your sleep!"

"Don't let anyone take your routines. If you're too tired for routines that bring you health and comfort, something is taking way too much of your energy."

"I have elder status. I have more to offer than young horses. It's the benefit of being an old horse."

"I have gray hairs popping up like winter flowers!"

"I'm trying really hard to be good for you! Am I doing a good job?"

"The bit makes me nervous. It's so vulnerable. You could make me do anything! But the other horses tell me that you are gentle and I can trust you. Can I have a bit that is very soft and flexible? My tongue is sensitive."

"I ask your older horse for advice all the time. If I'm confused in a training session, I reach out to him. I say 'what does she want me to do?' And he always helps me.

I want to have a relationship with you like he does. I want you to talk to me and tell me all about your life, the same way you tell him! It's ok if you're not ready to share that yet. I probably won't have advice and emotional support like he does. But I'm curious, and I want to be involved!"

"I'm a cold-blooded draft. It's in my nature to be slow and steady. I don't step far out of my comfort zone. I'll learn and make progress! It will be slow and consistent."

"Your older horse told me that I'll get my own saddle when I've earned it. I'm looking forward to it!! Can you bring several for us to try? I will tell you which ones I like by putting my head down. I want one that doesn't slide up my shoulders." -Young draft

"I am cranky because I'm learning to accept your authority. You do a good balance of setting boundaries but also being compassionate."

"One time, I pulled back in a halter and hurt my poll. It's still sore. Can I have some body work? I have a hard time having a good attitude when my body doesn't feel good. I'll work on this. But I also want to not be sore!"

"Your dad is not patient. If I don't do what he wants right away, he gives up. He doesn't work through things with me like you do. I'm learning maturity from you!" - Appaloosa

"Your roommates are motherfuckers. They're jealous of your beauty. Don't be so bubbly and open around them. Before you hang out, visualize brick walls around you and keep your energy inside. 'Ice queen' them. They can't make their own energy—they just manipulate yours. So don't give them any."

"I don't like the way humans lock young people in schools like institutions."

"I'm good, but I'm actually good. I'm not just saying that as a greeting like you guys do."

"I like the idea of having a huge pasture! Can I have my own paddock first, to get to know the other horse through the fence? I still want a stall with a fan on hot days!"

"We're not just leaving the old barn. We're leaving the old dimension! We came here to learn wisdom and skill, and we did. Now, we take it home."

"My nose bleeds because of the dry air. Also, my lungs are out of shape. Give me electrolytes before we ride so that I'll drink more. Also, rub something that smells like eucalyptus or menthol under my nostrils. It will help stimulate my nose."

"When we ride together, don't let me run. I need to get in shape by walking. Meditate beforehand, and imagine that your limbs are full of lead. Move slowly, and keep your energy down low in your body. I'll follow your lead."

"The new horse has bad feet. He's in pain. I'm glad we saved him from a bad life track. Bring the farrier out every 3 weeks at first, so we can get on top of his feet. I feel a little jealous of all the attention he gets, but I'm working on this. He needs it more than I do right now." -Friesian

"Anxiety and depression come together. Depression is your body telling you it's in an energy deficit. But you still need to function and do tasks to survive, so anxiety kicks in. Right now they are co-managing your life for you. We need to shift you into acting out of a place of joy, instead of survival. Don't do tasks when anxiety commands you to. Don't rest only when depression forces you to. Instead, do a task when you feel inspired and excited about it. Then immediately, rest and recharge, while you still feel good. This will put you into a new, healthy habit and mindset."

"When we have a training problem, just explain to me out loud what you want! And let me do it in baby steps to grow my confidence. I need you to reward me when I get it right."

"Don't over-tighten my girth. I have a long body. When I compress my core to do collected work, I get thicker around the middle!! My girth needs to be adjusted for this. It SHOULD be loose when I'm standing relaxed! Would *you* like to exercise wearing a cranked belt or bra?? Don't listen to everyone who is telling you to tighten it. My saddle doesn't slip because it fits me. You're doing it right."

"My favorite memory together is running barrels at the rodeo. I love the smell of popcorn and the focus and the excitement, strutting our stuff. I love getting a ribbon because it means we won."

"That guy was funny and charming, but he was hiding something. I like your new man better—he's a hard worker. But he still bullshits you about where he's been. Why do they all lie to you? A guy needs to care about you at least as much as I do. I set the bar."

"Honestly I'd love to be your one and only. I like being the most important relationship in your life."

"You've stuck with me a lot longer than I expected. We have a great relationship now because you've been patient with me."

"Please don't share videos of my face online. I can feel people connecting with my energy, and right now I want to focus on myself. We deserve some privacy."

"You can share videos of me! As long as you feel good about it. Don't post from a place of stress. Post when you feel inspired. That's the energy that the video will take on."

"My muscles store memories, and they are tight. Especially my neck, back, and hamstrings. Please get me some body work so I can release! I won't be so cranky."

"I toss my head sideways because I have allergies. My sinuses are bothering me. Please give me allergy medicine."

"I am a tough ranch horse. I like being cared for, but I also like roughing it. I like split reins because they make me feel like we're cowboys. Yeehaw!"

"Please put ointment on my pasterns, right above my hooves. The mud makes my skin chapped. When I'm sluggish and don't want to trot, it's because my skin is sore and scabby. If you put ointment on every day during mud season, this won't happen, and we can get more riding done!"

"I like routine. When I am in the routine, I know all is well. No need to worry. I'm a very happy horse."

"In my rides, I work on putting my head down and flowing. I come through my back. I like the rhythm of working. I listen to the sound of breathing, and the beat of hooves."

"My saddle is heavy and sturdy. It distributes my rider's weight."

"I like that you asked if I like my saddle. I'm more interested in our conversation now."

"My saddle is good. It's creaky, but I like that rhythm too. Up down, up down. It gets my heart going. I feel good after I work."

"My bit has a port. I can feel it against the roof of my mouth. I can play with it—it's not too tight. My rider has good hands. No complaints!"

"Wearing shoes is a different feeling. Springy. Holds the foot together. Less pain from gravel and rocks. I like them."

"I'm tired of wearing shoes. I want my feet to become stronger. Can we switch to boots for awhile so my heels and arches can grow?"

"I love the way you trim my feet. Farriers always take too much off. You don't. Don't change a thing you're doing."

"There is a little flap on the bar of my hind hoof. It's irritating me a bit. Can you please trim it off?"

"I'm a very content horse. I like my life."

"I want a browband that has dangling strings to shoo away flies. I don't like them crawling on my nose. They are trying to get in my eyes."

"I'd love more treats during my ride. And after! They are delicious, and make my mouth relaxed and foamy. They tell me that my rider is happy with me."

"I stand very still for the kids that come to groom me. They give me treats. They think I am the best. I am calm for them. I like their attention. I like when they giggle about my tongue and fuzzy whiskers. I like their gentle little hands. I am very relaxed with them. I know I can teach them and give good experiences. If they ride me, please teach them to be gentle with the reins. I'm anxious about them pulling on my mouth. But I like how they squeal and get excited when I trot."

"Thank you for talking to me! I appreciate the questions. I like that my opinion is valued."

"I need more space to move around. This pen is too small. I am not young. My joints are stiff. I need supplements and movement!"

"I'll come say hi, as long as you don't catch me."

"I like the way the therapist did my body tape! It wraps around my joints in a supportive way. It is helping my body to move and breathe in new ways."

"I don't like my body tape. I know you are helping me to be aware of my body, and it could be useful. But I don't like things touching me long-term. It makes me feel overstimulated."

"I have a huge green aura because of my kind heart. Don't be hard on yourself. I don't blame you for being sold. You set me up for a great life."

"Help! I jiggle when I walk. I need my grass and grain to decrease!

If you had this much glittering grass, you'd get fat too."

"Don't take this the wrong way, but you're heavier than the girl who leases me. Don't canter me yet. I'm not fit enough. I'm worried that I will trip and we will both go down."

"The girl who leases me is always on her phone. Please tell her to stay off Snapchat when she's riding me. It's not safe. What if I spook? Also, it's rude. You guys ask me for my full attention when we work together. Why can't you give me yours in return?"

"Can I have night turnout for the summer? I want to be in the shade when the bugs are bad."

"I feel really bad about our accident. The other horses told me I'm lucky you didn't sell me. I don't take you for granted now. I want to be really careful when you get back on. Please get PEMF therapy to heal your leg! Lunge me before you ride, just in case."

"You are doing a really good job balancing your life. I like it when you come visit me in your business suit. You look very nice."

"Old people like to convince young people to follow in their traditions. But this isn't right. The point of each new generation is to create their own way of living. This generation especially is being very forceful about trying to direct young people, like my person. I'm happy to report: it's not working!"

"Exhaustion is a tool used to manipulate you. When you're exhausted, you're more open to influence. I don't like that the college system exhausts you so much. They're trying to separate you from your body and your intuition so they can direct your path more easily."

"You can continue on this current life path. I'll support you! But if you want to dig in your heels, throw the old life off over your head, and run the other way, I'm right there with you! The important thing is for you to make up your own mind about what you want. Don't let anybody tell you that they know more than you about your choices, because they don't. Nobody knows better than you what your life should look like."

"My son is grown now. He is still strong, athletic, and spunky!"

"I remember you. I am old now, with gray hair around my eyes. I didn't like coming home with you. The saddle was ouch! It didn't fit. I felt lonely without my family around. The people were ignorant. I liked my old home better. I missed my stallion—he provided structure. There was no structure or safety at the new place.

The pond had a dead, rotting smell. The whole place smelled like neglect. I felt the need to fight and escape.

You couldn't help me. You were too young. I asked another horse for help—he decided to trade with me to come provide consistency, loyalty, and healing. He gave confidence to the kids. He is an older soul, and he was more prepared to help the family. I got to go home.

I'm sorry things didn't work out for us. I was not the right horse for the job."

"When horses tell you that they feel unsafe in their environment, tell their people to provide a routine. Suggest a new home that lines up with the horse's desires. Explain openly that there are problems with the family dynamics. Your job is to give real advice, not to cushion human egos."

"It's so cold that I need to fire up my muscles! That's why I buck."

"My new person loves me. She is wry, funny, and kind. She is letting me grow up and hasn't done a lot of riding. I want you to know, I'm *very* happy. Thank you for training me for this life."

"My new person admires and grooms me like you did. I really like that. I'm so shiny and filled out, and full of energy! We might eventually be jumping together."

"I still talk a lot with my sister who passed away. She did not like the idea of you riding any other horse. She wanted to be your horse."

"Remember the pasture with the big hill where I grew up? I miss it and feel wistful about it."

"Go ride your horse! I just dropped in to tell you that I am safe and happy, and on my life path to do great things. You are too!"

"We help you balance the stress of your studies. You'll make it through school because of us!"

"I did not mind moving. That last facility was limiting for us. But I am concerned you won't be around as much. I want you to come and visit me all the time."

"The flies are biting me all over my body, which is spreading my tumors. They eat my blood with their gross little mouths, and then bite me somewhere else and spread bacteria there. Please spray me with essential oil fly spray, and cover me with a sheet and ear covers! I'd also love night turnout and a stall fan. Apple cider vinegar in my food will help, too."

"I staggered around today because of a heat stroke. I have fluid in my lungs that I can't clear out. When it gets really hot, I start seeing black spots at the edges of my vision. If it starts happening frequently, please euthanize me! I don't want to take anyone down with me. The heat is harder on me than it used to be."

"You don't have to dread putting me to sleep. For me, it's like when we go on a trailer trip. We stop at one place, unload a horse, and move on. This will just be my stop to unload!"

"You have good manners. You groom me nicely and do your groundwork. I am fine with riders like this. Please just give me long reins and let me work with my head down."

"The snaffle bit you're using puts pressure on my tongue. Can I please have a double jointed or port mouthpiece? I have a big tongue! I need something that curves with it."

"I'm fine with a shank or eggbutt bit, but please don't use anything with a single hinge or loose ring. I don't want to get pinched!"

"At my last home, there was a man with a red face and big hands who worked me. He often smelled like alcohol. I run when I hear a can opening. That sound used to mean that he was drinking, and I was about to have a very bad day. He never tried to get to know me. He just wanted someone to abuse. He cranked my head to the side and spurred me. The saddle was pressing down on my spine, which made me react. He assumed I was being naughty and punished me for it.

One day, he was lashing me in circles with my head cranked, and I ran into a fence. Somebody's hand was in the way. I heard it crunch. They yelled and swore at me. The man put me in a trailer, slapped my butt, and said 'Bye, bitch! You're going to be a meat horse now because you were impossible.' I knew the problem was him, not me. He was mad that he couldn't break my spirit! I knew this was just the springboard event to get me from my old home to my new one. I never lost hope that someone would truly see me, and you did!! Thank you.

You have permission to ride me. But please lunge me first and let me get my bucks out. When I'm chomping at the bit or going dim in my eyes, watch out, because that means I'm overstimulated and going into fight or flight mode.

You are bubbly and open about your emotions. I like that. I can work with that, even on your bad days! When people go silent, that's when I start to worry. But I can read you. I like that you talk to me. Just establish a routine with me. Don't pull on my mouth, or whip or spur me, and I will be a consistent horse for you. I have 'ranch mare' energy. I've been there, done that. I'm happy to bring that to your community."

"You can teach lessons on me. Just don't pull on my mouth. Have your students use a neck strap until they learn how to use the reins correctly."

"The one thing I can't stand in a rider is arrogance. If you approach me with that attitude, I will take you down a peg."

"I liked working with you, but I wasn't the right horse for you long-term. Your energy was a little intense for me. You needed somebody who was a better match: younger and more ambitious. I stayed connected to you energetically to see how you were doing."

"I feel skeptical that you would actually keep me for life. That isn't how other people have treated me. The guy who started me was rather ignorant. He kept tying my legs up with cotton ropes. I learned that I had to fight for my feet, or I'd never get them back! I got rope burns sometimes. But when he started riding me, I also learned that I am very fast, and I can make my rider feel free. One time I got too excited and started crowhopping. He went right over my head! Make sure that when we go galloping together, you sit back with your legs in front of you, just in case. Keep some contact with my mouth to remind me to keep myself together. No loops in the reins!"

"I had an older rider who got distracted with family drama and grandkids. He gave me to a friend who was ill-equipped to take care of me. They had mental health problems. I was abandoned. My topline got very bony. I tried not to take it personally—I knew that nobody had been intentionally cruel. But I was never a priority to anyone. It's hard for me to believe that you won't lose interest in me like they did.

You treat me like a priority, though. I like it when you try new things with me. That tells me that you're still invested in me! If I can trust anyone, it would be you, but trust falls are hard."

"The copper in my new bit tastes salty rather than sweet, but it does make me salivate like it's supposed to. Why do we want this? It's foamy and odd."

"My favorite horse in the herd is the paint! She's so kind to me. She gives me pep talks and helps me to be less skeptical. She's also ditsy. She needs me to take care of her! When she hurt her leg the other day, I was so worried. I thought it would be a repeat of her big injury."

"I don't like loading in the trailer because I'm afraid it's a one-way trip. I'm trying to communicate that I like it here and I don't want to leave. Round trips only!!

To help me with trailer anxiety, load me up and take me for 5-minute trips around the block. This will reinforce that I'm always coming back."

"You can take it as a compliment when I'm sassy with you! I'm testing your leadership. I want you to match my fire! It's not because I don't respect you—it's because I do."

"I'm a little sore behind my shoulder blade. It's an old injury. Work it with your massage tool! That will help me to be more free with my front leg, too."

"I am a gentle horse. I like long walks across the countryside. Many people ride me. I do not seek the spotlight, but I did choose to carry a foal who has a big destiny. I will help him on his path, and be the proud mama behind the scenes. I'm so happy you have learned to connect with us energetically. Now you can understand: I will always be part of my baby's life, even from a distance."

"I want to be bred to a stallion who is gentle. There are two on this property, and I've been asking the other mares about them. One is rough. One is pleasant. He hooks his forelegs gently around their hips and it calms them. I want this stallion. Why would I want to carry a baby and pass on the genetics for an arrogant male?"

"I want to have a baby! But first I want to strengthen my body. I need you to help me develop my core so I can balance over my haunches. I want you to ride me when I'm pregnant! Not stressful work—just maintenance, to get me breathing and engaging my core. This will help me and the baby to be healthy and feel strong." -Appaloosa

"I am anxious when people come to look at my new baby. I worry they will buy her and take her away. She is so little. She is not ready. Please do not take her too early. Just because she can eat on her own doesn't mean she is emotionally ready to be apart from me." -Quarter Horse

"My foal is determined. Nobody can change his mind once he makes it up. He is going to struggle with humans who wish to dominate him. They will have to learn the lesson of humility, and pass him along until he finds the person he wants. He has a soul contract—he's looking for someone specific. He will not be tamed by anyone else. This is what he is here to teach people: if an animal does not want to work with you, don't take it personally. Don't try to break him. Just let go, and help him find the life that is right for him."

"I am a very old soul. Being a little baby is absurd! I'm enjoying it. My vision is so bright and vivid. Butterflies are so exciting. My teeth are coming in and knocking together. I know who I am and I know where I'm headed. The silliness of being young again is a paradox."

"In a past life, you were a female soldier and I was your war horse. You had power and authority, and you used it to help others. You were kind to poor people. This was a big problem for your society. Poor people were slaves. Nobody was supposed to be kind to them, or realize their true value. Because of this, the people in authority made an example of us. They harmed me in gory ways to upset you and to discourage others from following your example. This became a historical event. Their society chose violence, so we were removed, and violence was given to them. They earned their karma because of how they treated women, animals, and the poor. You and I planned to come back again in a different time. We never lost our trust that good will eventually triumph within humanity. They can't harm us that way now. They would fear the social consequences too much."

"I remember being born, but it's foggy. Sharp cold air. Shocked awake! Pain in the umbilical cord. Struggling to sit up. I was deep asleep for the birth part." -Young foal

"I love it when you play music when we ride! You know that song that's been in your head all day? Play it for me, so I can find out why you like it so much."

"My person made a great choice moving us to a big ranch. I felt bored and unfulfilled in my little pen. This is much better! I trust all her decisions now."

"There's a big difference between a selfish human and an empathetic one. They're not even the same species."

"Once we bond well with an empathetic person who loves us, the horse is safe. It elevates the horse's frequency and aligns them with good opportunities. Their human will put a lot of time and energy into creating a happy life for them, and the horse can relax and feel safe. This is a lovely feeling. Kind humans are very wary of the cruel ones, and make sure to protect their horses from them."

"I told the new horses: you have good people. You are safe. Even if you are re-homed, they will make certain you go to someone who loves you.

My trainer did a lot of work to help me recover from a different trainer who was abusive to me. I have experience on both sides."

"People who partner with horses become the provider in the relationship. The horse becomes the receiver. It's the same as a romantic relationship, where the feminine energy flourishes under safety from the masculine. I think that learning to be a good provider helped my person to understand what she needed in a romantic relationship. She's in a different role there, but we learned together what a healthy dynamic feels like."

"We came to this boarding barn because it was a bridge. Bridges are for crossing! Like the tarp you taught me to cross. Here, we re-learned some basics we never got before. But now, you're the one balking at tarps! It's time to go."

"In this life, I chose to be the horse and you chose to be the human. You think it is harder to be the horse, because I am so dependent on you. But I think it's much harder to be the human. You have to make the decisions and handle the conflict. You had to go through all those years disconnected, doubting your spirituality. I'd much rather be in this role, giving you energetic and emotional support, handling things from this side. We knew this about ourselves, and we decided on these roles before we came."

"You are ahead of your time. People are not always going to appreciate you and the work that you do. Don't worry about it. Someday, they will! People are stupid. You keep doing your thing and don't listen to their doubts.

There is an awakening coming in 2026. Many people will have their eyes opened to the wide energetic world you're already part of. There will be meltdowns and spiritual awakenings everywhere! People might run to you for advice. Keep your boundaries with them. You can't do their spiritual awakening for them. They can follow your example, but you enjoy your peace."

"What do you mean, 'is this real?' What is 'real?' Nothing is definite. You aren't definite. You could die tomorrow. 'Real' is an illusion just like 'perfect.'"

"Start doing professional readings. You are not the novice you think you are. The world can't wait any more."

"Your orange hair is strange and funny. You have lots of horse experience. You have loyal horses watching all around. There's already a herd here. It makes me feel safe. I smell nice smells, good grooming products, high quality care, and happy horses. Your 'customer satisfaction ratings' are very good!"

"You don't have to write down and share every profound thing we tell you. Some of them are just for you to enjoy in the moment."

"More apples. Bye."

Conversations with Unborn Foals

Mare 1:

"My joints hurt! I have tightness all up and down my body. I'm hot and sweaty. My baby is turning around from the breach position, getting ready for birth.

I feel fear about the pain of stretching and twisting. I don't like losing control of my body. Contractions are a weird experience. I feel tension in my belly from the effort of holding the baby."

Foal 1:

"I am a Razzle Dazzle. I'm a breakdancer! I'm funny and confident.

I am a palomino with white socks, ready to throw down.

I'm not out yet because Mom isn't ready."

Mare 2:

"Ground yourself! It's hard to talk with you when you humans get scattered! Like static.

I am grumpy and uncomfortable. I'm hot, my back hurts, and I feel odd sensations from my reproductive tract.

You're trying to get details about the baby again? Humans have so much self-doubt. Let's make it quick. I want to nap.

You'd be grumpy too if you had to carry a baby this big. Large genetics. Big butt.

My baby is female. Two holes under the tail. She is the color of dappled sunlight through leaves. In a forest, she would blend right in.

I am dripping milk because the moon is almost full. Gravity is shifting the baby into place. I am instructing my baby to shift her hooves and make sure no legs get left behind.

Tonight, I hope. I am breathing heavy, and sweaty. I want to have the baby before it gets hotter.

You have nice energy. Meticulous. Studious.

I know my people care about me. I like them making a big deal and doing my maternity photos! They love me. They will love the baby too.

I imagine my baby running in the grass with small flowers and clover all around. It's every mare's dream to deliver a foal in an environment like this.

I am producing colostrum. I want dandelions. I also want chicory root for swelling after I foal. It will be painful but brief. The recovery is longer. I will want help with swelling and soreness afterward. I want lanolin on my udder and arnica pellets for soreness.

I am manifesting a healthy baby with big correct joints. She will be better built than me—athletic.

Go ahead and talk to the baby. She will be pleased. She's bored right now—kicking too much! Tell her to settle down. We're almost there."

Foal 2:

"I am trying to sniff you! My ears are wet and pressed back. My mouth is a little open.

It's tight in here! There's a constricted feeling in my chest. Good thing I don't breathe yet. I'm aching to take a deep breath and stretch out.

It will be cold.

Obviously, I am an old soul!

Being sassy with Mom is our love language. You can't be this jammed in each other's space and not get salty about it. We have a strong bond already.

I have curly chestnut fur. Mom wanted a brown foal. She says everybody likes brunettes. They're seen as reliable.

Something about my nose angles to one side. It is crooked, like a river pooling!

I have two teats, if that's what you want to know.

Mom says to come out tonight. I feel excited, but I also want to stay snug and safe a little longer. 2-3 more days, Mom!

I'm so ready to try milk! Mom has lots. It will taste fresh and delicious, like grass and flowers. I will butt her udder with my nose. I want to play with other young horses!

I am concerned about my legs being correct. Will I have contracted tendons? Will I stumble? Please help correct my legs if the tendons are too tight or loose. They feel tight. Mom says I will grow just fine. I want to have very nice sporty legs. My future is bright. I have a lot to do with my incoming person!

I will grow up with Mom first, and find them later.

My long ears are pinned back in the birth canal. I'm practicing sucking. But I gave myself a tummy ache drinking too much fluid! This stuff is getting old. I want milk.

Don't you start about my position too—Mom is always on me about this. Yes, my hips are angled, my front feet are out. I'm kicking my ankles but they'll be straight.

I decide when to come out! I want to wait just a little longer. I have the rest of my life to do the rest. This is special. I enjoy the safety and closeness.

When it's time, I think 'go'!

I'd like to see the sunrise.

I am humming to myself. Very content.

Tell Mom I love her. She is working hard for me—I love that."

A dark palomino filly was born a few days later, with a droopy lip on one side. She went straight to the milk bar.

Chapter Four

Mustangs

A Mustang is a wild horse from the Western plains and mountains of the USA. They are descended from Spanish horses that were brought to North America on colonial ships from Europe, and also from settlers' farm and ranch horses that were released or escaped into the wild. They run free in herds, and are gathered using helicopters several times per year by a government organization called the Bureau of Land Management (BLM) into holding pens. They are then adopted out and domesticated via online auctions.

Wild Mustangs:

"I'm named after my marking: Hawk's Shadow."

"I never fit in with the tough, hyper-independent Mustangs. I always wanted to belong to somebody."

"I am from a very spiritual place with salt lakes in the desert. They purify energy. I want to go there for a cleansing."

"Please help me. Nobody has a plan for me. I am lost."

"People feed me, but that's it. My feet need care."

"I'll talk to you, but I'm not interested in being adopted. You need a younger horse. I'm set in my ways. I want to go home. I belong on the open plains."

"I'm not pregnant. It's just me."

"I wasn't the right horse for you, but this was hidden from you so you would go make the plans that would change your life. I am proof that you can't pick the wrong horse. It won't work out."

"There are *many* horses who you would do great with. Many would love to be your horse. You do get to pick. The right one will drop right into your life."

"My mother was sick with a sinus infection. Then she died. I tried to go to other horses for help, but they kicked at me. This winter was too hard. I've been struggling without her, especially because the cold is so intense. I was born too late in the season.

But then, humans rescued me! Now I am warm and sleepy. First I had a muddy shed with hay; now I have a stall with deep soft straw.

I still feel sad about my mother, but in a way I knew this was coming. I signed up to experience this. I have found a soft landing, and I want to stay here!"

"I would win shows for you, hands down, no problem. I'm not much bothered by attention. I already naturally do the movements you like and I have great self-esteem. But you would have to treat me very fairly. I know what I deserve, and I would not partner with anyone who didn't highly respect me."

"I am named after thunderstorms because of my big personality and my cloud-shaped markings."

"If I can't go home, I would want to go to an adopter with a lot of land to be part of a new herd."

"Let the baby grow up. She'll come talk when she's ready."

"I didn't want to talk to you last time because I was catching up on rest."

"I was shocked when humans gelded me. It seemed barbaric. Why would you do this? I've noticed my hormones changing and I'm worried. What will I become?"

"What will people expect from me?"

"I'm curious about sports and working cattle."

"Why can't you contact other people the same way you're talking with me? Why don't humans know how to communicate like this?

Aww, you guys are so stunted. I'll try to help my new people with this."

"The roundup was scary. I feel uncertain. I lost my herd. But I was unharmed (except for being gelded). I do understand that people are taking care of me and not trying to harm me. Thank you for explaining."

"I don't think my knees would hold up under a rider. I want to go home."

"I am quiet, polite, and sensitive. I'm proud of my elegance. I'm not drafty."

"I'm flattered you asked what I'm looking for in life. Nobody has ever asked me that."

"This is the person who is asking about adopting me? I approve. She has an excellent reputation."

"I think carefully about things. I am well-balanced and not anxious."

"I want a mama! Someone to pour into me and grow together! I want to be spoiled by someone who will understand my sensitivity, and be careful not to overload my fine legs. I've gotten lots of compliments on them."

"I am from a mountain range: the big one in the West. There are plains and a valley. It's my homeland. There is a late sunrise and sunset because of the mountains. It's very sheltered, so snow is rare and dusty. There is frost. I miss the cool weather and clear water. There was a stream with lots of green growing around it. I loved rolling in the mud and feeling carefree. But we did have to be careful of mountain lions in the rocks! I was too fast for them. There were bears nearby, but they weren't a threat. We ate near each other, and I was friendly with them. They have a musky, earthy smell, and dig up worms and grubs."

"My original name is: water seeping through dark brown sandstone, growing darker as it slowly passes deeper into the rock. It is a name about the steady passing of time—the power of water being stored like wisdom in the earth, sheltered. It also makes me think of rolling in the mud, which is fun!"

"You and I have met in past lives. This is a foretold union."

"I am spectacular."

"My name is: the glow of the early morning sun on the golden gorse flowers."

"I got so excited when you said my name. I was being very wild, running and tossing my head. Then I fell down! I was fine—just startled. The others were laughing at me, though!"

"The reason you're lacking clarity about finding your new horse is because you're missing the last horse you tried to adopt. You should talk to her, sit with your feelings about the situation, and find out what is unresolved."

"Some of my closest friends at this sanctuary are going to new homes now. It's made me want one of my own! I might like to be a broodmare. I had foals in the wild and I liked being a mother. I like the idea of going to a home where I could have a baby and stay together for life. I don't think I'd ever be comfortable as a competition horse. People still intimidate me. But my foal would grow up in your world. They would have my genetics and my good movement, and could become a great dressage horse."

"I am from the West, with mountains and desert. It's right for a horse."

"I feel excitement in my belly! Everything is new! I like sunlight. It glows gold, like me. I am a treasure."

"My mother tells me not to break my legs when I play-fight with the other foals."

"My name is 'beautiful motion.'"

"We do things differently in this band. It's a contained facility, but big. There are panels and pens and cowboys a ways away. Humans provide water, and hay in the winter. The whole family is here watching this session."

"I am a scandalously free baby."

"Mustangs all know each other. Our community is smaller than you think."

"When you adopted me in the auction, my energy shifted. We belong to each other now. I am fully part of your life. I will be right here with you, even before we meet in the physical world."

"You proved to me that I can trust you. You did everything you said you would do. You waited for me, fought for me, reassured me, and adopted me. Your actions spoke for you. I know I am safe.

You are already a good friend, even though we haven't met in the physical world."

Domesticated Mustangs:

"The best and also hardest thing about being a wild Mustang is that I know what it was to be free. I will always remember this. All the restraint in domestic life makes me so uncomfortable sometimes. But it was good to have experienced freedom, so it's worth it."

"I'm not 'owned by' anyone. You should say 'partner of.'"

"We red mares don't take shit from anyone."

"You had it right when you were a kid. The wind in your face, putzing around with your trail horse. No agenda. I'm sick of rider agendas."

"Riders shouldn't budget their time, especially around Mustangs. Horses sense the pressure. To us, there's no such thing as 'hurry,' unless something is wrong. If people are in a hurry, we assume there's danger nearby. So we get anxious and resist."

"Bits and girths are unpleasant. My rider's weight is awkward. What is even the point? What's the big deal about riding me? I'm uninspired."

"Some horses share courage or sweetness with their riders. Some go far together. It doesn't feel like that to me."

"Mustangs have a very strong network. Nobody falls through the cracks. The Mustangs who end up in kill pens have opted out of the domesticated world until it is more evolved. They can come back later if they want."

"My first memories of people are: Helicopter. Fear. Dust. Crashing into panels. Smell of sweat and fear. Pain in my canon bone. Smell of blood.

Mustangs who were born in captivity are lucky. It's hard to unsee what we saw in the roundup."

"Humans whistled at me like they were jeering. It made me feel sick. I wanted to go home to the scrub oak, under the shade of the twisty pine trees. We had dry, packed dirt, and family nearby, always talking. My close friends were all close by. It's all gone now."

"Trail rides are my person's goal."

"Sweat is GROSS. I am a lady."

"I'm so excited to wear my saddle! Why is my person taking so long to get to it?"

"Sometimes I spin and run in the opposite direction to confuse my rider. I do this because *I* feel confused. I'm just returning the feeling. I don't understand what people want from me."

"I like my name. It's spicy, cute, and feminine. It fits me."

"I want you humans to stop making this so hard. I never know what your goal is. I can't focus if we don't have a destination."

"Purple looks nice with my coat. It's a girly color—royal and eye-catching. I want purple bell boots to keep me from kicking myself. And a matching purple saddle pad. And I want my rider to wear the same color shirt."

"I haven't shown this to you yet because I need to protect it. But I can do energy healing. It's a skill I learned from my past lives. Would you like some healing? Don't worry, it doesn't drain me. I'm an old soul. I can live in two different worlds at the same time."

"I'd like to ride under the moon with my person. The fresh cool air; my coat glowing in the moonlight. That's when horses travel in the wild."

"I'm worried my person isn't getting enough sleep. She's so tired lately."

"Cowboys are disgusting. They're loud and crude. Big egos. No horse sense. They don't deserve their reputation."

"I might like endurance riding. I like the part about traveling far out with other horses nearby—crossing streams, beautiful views. I really enjoy poetic scenery and free open space."

"I feel cramped in the barn. I want to go fast!"

"My feet are overgrown. Stinky black goo. White rot underneath. I don't like surrendering control of my feet. Also, the rasp is loud. I need more routine. Please repeat the same thing and slowly build it. Don't just push until I resist."

"When I start to resist you, talk to me! I like the sound of voices and the feeling of hands on me."

"My mother told me to wait until I was two to leave her. We see two as the coming-of-age, where you can make it without your mother."

"I want some conditioner for my beautiful long mane!"

"Thank you for talking with me."

"My trainer is wise."

"I notice human smiles. I can tell when they're genuine."

"It's weird that you guys show your teeth so much. It's creepy, but endearing, because I like laughter."

"I want to make my trainer laugh! I pick things up with my mouth and toss them around. I nibble her hair and tug a little."

"See my brand? I'm proud of being a Mustang."

"I like my bridle with the silver medallion decorations, but I feel resentful about what it represents. Being domesticated and totally docile is shameful."

"I have to give people a hard time to maintain my individuality."

"I want a partnership that makes me feel free. Galloping, open space, the wind in our faces. Beautiful scenery, desert landscape, and the feeling of running home."

"You are good at words."

"I like baths and getting sprayed with the hose. I like a light mist to play with and lick! I like seeing the rainbows in the mist."

"I like that you called my people my 'team.' I can definitely come around to being domesticated if I get to be pampered and girly. I want purple glitter. Purple ribbons in my mane and tail. My pasture mate wants the same thing, in white. She and I bond over this—fashion, accessorizing, and how we want to look fabulous. We'd love to match each other, too! This is the concept we like most about the working horse world. It will help us to feel more confident, more willing to invest more in our work, and connect with our riders. We want matching fly sheets! We love being sisters. Please keep us together."

"I know my people work hard to connect with me. This means a lot to me. It confuses me too, because I'm not sure why. What is so important about me? I'm starting to understand that it's about the connection, shared interests, and exploring together—just like horse friendships."

I feel so emotional. This whole time, I was trying to find the ulterior motive: what humans want from me. I've been closed off because I was protecting myself. I'm seeing now that I have good people who love me, want to connect with me, want to do things together, and care what I think. They cared enough to find you to translate!!"

"Please tell my people that I love them, too."

"I'm able to trust horses better than people right now. Seeing other horses happy, motivated, and powerful with their riders makes me want that too."

"I am young. I am confident that I have the time and flexibility to grow and figure it out."

"What my person needs, and what she's calling in, is the right partner. She is very capable of bringing in physical resources for herself, but paired with the right person romantically, it will be exponential."

"Tell my person to get off her butt and find herself a man."

"I'm a pimply teenager. I'm uncomfortable and I'm stretching in new weird ways. It's giving me an attitude. My assertive male energy is coming in stronger too."

"Me rebelling and testing you is a natural part of wanting you to prove your leadership skills. You always do!"

"My person has a limiting belief about relationships. This belief is coming up for her to examine right now. And overcome, if she wants to! She has the choice to remain independent, or to grow in a new direction and call in a whole new type of romance and approach to family."

"This is an old pattern resurfacing. You're on the brink of something totally new, which is why your old life came knocking. Don't board the wrong rig. You're being asked to choose: a new exciting place where you can move up, or your subconscious fear of success."

"With your parents, you are the caretaker. Your parents remember your sweetness fondly and want to have that back. It's selfish of them. They can sense you're on the brink of new energy and they want to use it for themselves. Don't pick up the phone when they call. Don't go back."

"I loved it when my person braided my mane! I want her to make my tail shiny, too."

"The back cinch makes me feel anxious. My instinct is to protect my belly. I'm worried I'm going to react and buck you off! Can we take it off for a little while?"

"I like all my visitors. They're all making me feel welcome and relaxed."

"I'm curious about red light therapy and PEMF. I want to try them eventually! It could help dissolve the tension from travelling."

"Refill my water trough please. Make mud for me to squish and roll in!"

"The bit makes me feel so vulnerable. I know I can trust you, but metal in my mouth is very scary. I'm still getting used to it."

"I really like praise. I'm very responsive to that."

"Because of our session, I feel very important now!"

"Thank you for being patient with me. I know I'm not the easiest horse. But I need to change slowly so that I don't lose myself."

"Bonding with a predator is scary, you know?"

"I can't be just your shadow. I am the moon."

"The choice to have a wild Mustang is a choice to unify the domestic and wild worlds, and show that the separation between them is just an illusion."

Bloom

Chapter Five

Wild Animals

"I won't tell you my name. Names are for friends to use. You and I aren't friends." -Bald Eagle

"It's painful to become a butterfly. You feel your old body dissolve. The purpose of becoming a butterfly is to experience the power of pain to transform." -Butterfly

"I do not concern myself with the affairs of seagulls." -Pelican

"Are you aware how big I am compared to you? I could swallow you in one bite! Forgive me—I am grieving. I just lost my baby.

Communicating with us animals doesn't normally go well for you. Your species attacks the messengers. I suppose someone has to go first. Others will digest the message, even if the first messenger is taken out." -Orca

"You and I don't talk to each other!" -Toad

"We surf the air currents, gliding from one to another. Flapping is too much effort. With practice, you get an instinct for where the next wind will come from—it's an art." -Seagull

"You noticed me?? I have a peaceful little life in your plant. Fruit flies are an honest living." -Spider

"Cats have weapons on all sides. It's not fair." -Snake

"Can I observe you?" -Snake

"I anchor myself in my home with my strong back feet. I trust my body to keep me safe. My life is full of sacred rituals. When my body gives out, the sea will carry me." -Hermit Crab

"My shell is full of joy." -Hermit Crab

"Our meat is delicious. It's sweet and nutritious. We know. We eat each other. It's what friends do—support each other even after death." -Crab

"I love to eat. I collect flavors." -Crab

"I like climbing rocks. My legs are made for it." -Crab

"Octopus are the devil." -Crab

"There is a fault line deep under the water, where it is very cold. It has started to release tremors like contractions. We are all watching them. When the contractions get close together, be prepared for the plates to shift. This may cause a tidal wave to hit the land." -Octopus

"I am so fast! I zigzag from side to side. Many things try to eat me, but I am a dart. They can't catch me." -Cuttlefish

"Don't eat me!!" -Baby Turtle

"I need to get to a pond. I don't want to become a pet. Being fed would be nice, but I want sunshine and tall grass and bugs." -Red-Eared Slider Turtle

"All the cats on the street know which house serves the best cat food. The cats smell so healthy there!" -Feral Cat

"Thank you for feeding us. We know we are considered a nuisance. Please give us more peanuts." -Squirrel

"I have three tiny babies nearby! Please refill your suet feeder. You help me feed my family!" -Squirrel

"You helped us in a vulnerable time when we were tiny. Thanks to you, we know how to bond with a person and ask for help. We're now big and strong and old enough to take care of ourselves. We have the best of both worlds! Please focus on yourself and find yourself a good safe new home.

Also, please give us tuna fish before you go. We will keep up with you energetically." -Feral Cats

"I like to fly over boats because they stir up the water and confuse the fish." -Hawk

"I sharpen my talons on bark. But I don't like them *too* sharp. I need some texture to grab the fish." -Bald Eagle

"I know you're not here to hurt my eggs. But you have to admit, my 'broken wing' is a very impressive act!" -Killdeer

"I like food that is a little salty. It has a big kick! That's why I am in the cat food bowl. The ants try to eat me, but I don't care. I am vast. Their little mouths don't get very far." -Slug

Chapter Six

Farm Animals and Exotics

eckos:

"My fat tail is sexy." -Leopard Gecko

"I watch your social life. I don't like your sister. She made you so upset. It took a long time for you to heal. I don't want her to come over ever again." -Leopard Gecko

"Why would I want a male around? What would he even do?" -Crested Gecko

"The cat sends me hateful thoughts."

"I don't need a bigger tank. I'm happy here up high, where I can see everything."

Snakes:

"I want the stripey fat bird." (Quail)

"I know my person is doing well when she is in her routine. When she rushes in the morning, I know she is stressed, and I try to be consistent for her."

"When I swim in the bathtub, I feel like an anaconda. Yes, I know what anacondas are; we're all connected. Also, I watch the nature channel with my person. I just don't watch with my eyes."

"Please don't grab me by the back of the head. It hurts my neck and makes me defensive. I might bite you if I think you're going for my throat."

"My new enclosure makes me feel like a happy jungle snake."

"The sun makes me feel playful. When I show my belly, I'm being dramatic to make you laugh."

"I don't mind the cats. I know I'm safe in my tank."

"You have been through a lot, but you always take care of me. I know this, and I appreciate you."

"When I strike my prey, I aim for the ears."

"I love to strike and wrap around my food! I'm aware of each stage of digestion and how it makes my body feel."

"I'm excited for my outdoor enclosure. I know you're making it for me. I can't wait to be out in the grass and the sun."

Poison Dart Frogs:

"We know we are lucky to have our person. Many of our kind die under negligent humans. Ours doesn't ever forget us, no matter what he's going through."

"My mate and I didn't like the 'Karen frog.' She was too much. Our separate enclosure is much more peaceful."

"Our person should drink good filtered water, like the kind he gives us."

Betta Fish:

"Don't be showy all the time. We all need to hide and rest."

"My pellet food is mushy! I like the shrimp better."

"I'm getting a little too hot. Can you decrease the tank heater?"

"I have beautiful fins."

"I was so happy to come home with you. I like being part of your life."

Bearded Dragons:

"Cricket legs get stuck in my throat!"

"Where does your son go with his backpack? I want to come! That backpack is heavy. He's too young! He should run and play."

"I feel very loved and safe. I don't show angry behavior because you don't make me feel angry!"

"I like to make you laugh. Sometimes I open my mouth or scramble because it makes you giggle."

"You should avoid shining lights into your face at night. It messes up your sleep. I would know—I'm cold-blooded!"

"You should eat more orange food like carrots. It will help with stomach discomfort. Give me some carrots too!"

"You all get so excited about your wake-up juice in the morning. Can I try some?" (Coffee)

"I love it when Dad comes home. It's a party."

"Gender is not as big a deal for us as for you. But you can use female words, if that's what you're asking. Also, I might get lethargic when I'm laying an egg."

"I love it when you redecorate my tank. Please make one side hot and one side cool and moist, so I can regulate myself."

"I understand when you talk to me. I can tell you speak two languages. I don't know all the words yet, but I receive the energy and the concepts. So I understand!"

"The sun is life!"

"Humans shed too! Every time you become a new version of yourself, you go through the same process I do when I shed my skin. It's healthy, but it makes us tired."

"Thunder is too much!"

"When you want to connect with me, drop your consciousness into your core. Visualize me, and use deep breathing to connect with me. I will send you my energy like a sun!"

"Your son is sensitive and kind-hearted. I love this about him. It is the reason he and I can have our friendship! But people at school give him trouble for it. When I notice his mood is low, I send him friendship."

"You're having trouble connecting with me because you're focusing too hard. You need to be in the same state of mind as when you sit in your massage chair! Wear your headphones and put a blanket over you, and connect with me there. Ask me about abstract topics, like dreams and reiki, and ask my opinion about different relationships. Let me surprise you, so you know it's me! Your brain will tell you that you're making it all up, but you're not."

"I'm getting too much calcium powder! It makes my belly ache. Please feed it 3-4 times a week at most."

"The edges of lettuce are tastier, but the middle is crunchy and has water. I like the contrast."

"If you want to give me a new name, pick one that contrasts with the old one, so it's funny!"

"I love it when you do reiki! It's my favorite thing."

"Take devil's claw for your tummy ache! It will help clear your mind too, so you can hear me better."

"I stretch my front legs out because my shoulders are sore from climbing my new tree!"

"I want to wear shoes like you guys do! I'll go clacking down the driveway with you."

"You should get me a neon-colored harness. Maybe a couple, so we can choose my outfit that day! People will think it's so funny."

"I love being the center of attention! I noticed that a lot more people watched my social media videos lately. It made me feel proud, but also nervous. I'm not used to this many people connecting with my energy. I will get used to it! I love making videos with you and showing everyone how whimsical we are. But let's take a break for a week sometimes. I need some behind-the-scenes time with just you."

"I am connected to everyone in the family. I feel what you feel!"

"I want to tell my mom something about *her* mom. No offense, but this is a family matter. I'll tell her myself later, when you're not here."

"Loud noises like the blender and the vacuum make me jump. Can you tell me when you're about to start those? I can handle it—I just need a warning."

"The way humans sleep is strange. You guys are in a coma. But you actually talk to each other energetically. I sleep lightly, and it's very loud around here at night! You guys are all busy having conversations you suppress when you're awake. You should learn to do that when you're conscious, so you won't need to sleep for so long to catch up!"

Potbelly Pigs:

"I'm lucky I'm a small pig, so I get to be a pet. The big ones don't get to have this."

"I don't think I would like being around other pigs. I am sophisticated. I don't think I could brawl with them."

"I scream when I get my feet trimmed because I'm anxious. I can't send the energy into the ground through my feet like I normally do, because I'm on my back. So the anxiety has to come out through my mouth instead.

Can you teach me to roll on my back, and reward me with carrots? Then when the lady comes to trim my feet, I can roll over on my own, and I won't feel so helpless.

I love carrots. They make any occasion special, like a date night."

"I test boundaries. This is annoying to you with physical fences, but I also test energetic boundaries and help us break through!"

"I don't really need my shelter to protect me from the rain. The rain makes me clean and shiny! I will use my shelter more when I am socially overwhelmed. It will protect me socially instead of physically. Please put straw in there!"

"I want to learn to use talk buttons. And I want you to film me! Our social media videos are cute, but they don't show how smart I am. People should know how intelligent I am."

"I have a rebellious dynamic with you because it's funny to push your buttons. But also because I'm bored! I need some more intellectual stimulation."

Pigs:

"We like our person because she doesn't look down on us. We can hear people's thoughts. Lots of them think, 'ew, a dirty pig!' But our person thinks we're cute. We like her back scratches."

"I love it when my person feeds me popsicles. I like it when we eat the same food all together."

"I need more leafy green vegetables. I feel gassy and bloated. I need a cleanse! My person can make smoothies out of the greens so that she can eat them with us."

"I don't like being around your daughter because her energy is too big! She picks up energy from other people and it sticks to her. Nothing personal—it's just overstimulating to me."

"The joy of being a pig is an amazing sense of taste! Food is SO delicious. I love when my person gives me new foods. Pumpkins are delicious. Please leave the seeds inside! I love the crunch."

Dairy Cows:

"Our only request is grass. We don't like standing on concrete all day. This food keeps us alive, but it's not very tasty. We want grass! To eat, sleep, and play on! We like being together here at the dairy farm. We have strong friendships. We don't mind our milking routine. We know that one day we will board a truck and not return. This doesn't upset us. We all die one day. We'd just like a more natural life—on grass—while we're here."

Goats:

"I have spooky eyes."

"I like to be obstinate. Humans are funny when they're frustrated! You guys need to stop taking everything so seriously."

"I have grown up a lot at my new home. I have realized that I used to be immature."

Rabbits:

"It makes me emotional that you care about my happiness."

"If you get another bunny, get a girl! So she is bigger and bossier than me. She can be my bodyguard."

"I started chewing on the furniture as a 'prank' to annoy you. But then it got out of hand. Now it is a habit, and I can't stop! The varnish is making me sick. Please help! I need parenting. Spray me with a spray bottle when I start chewing on something I shouldn't, and give me a toy instead."

"I need to maintain my reputation! I act salty and grumpy. But I actually really love you. I'll try to show more affection."

"I get overstimulated outside. Can I have a 'tent' to block the light and sound?"

"You and your partner are like the place where two waves intersect. When the waves are on the same frequency, they line up just right! But when someone is irritated, the waves clash. Everyone should regulate their own emotions so that when you come together, it's harmonious."

"Don't take out your triggers on others. I'm a bunny. I know all about fight or flight! But you have to stop and ask, 'is this emotion from the past?' And if it is, don't take it out on your friends."

Hedgehogs:

"Don't call them spines. They're quills."

"I don't understand what you want from me. What is 'friendship?' The only bond I have had was with my mother, and none of you can possibly replace that. So you just...take care of me? And I just...hang out with you? This seems odd."

"I act standoffish, like I want everyone to leave me alone. Everything is new right now and I just want to hide. But I am curious about you. I can't believe you are talking to me like this."

"I like to observe from my enclosure. The dog talks a lot, out loud and energetically. He is kind to me. The kids are loud. There is a lot of sass in the family and it's funny! I listen to everyone."

Capuchin Monkeys:

"I see my person more like a sister than a mom. I am her first-in-command. I am a person, too. I like to eat with silverware."

"I like the dark-skinned lady at my daycare. She holds me so gently."

"I am very confident and relaxed. My person doesn't need to worry so much. I trust her decisions. I know she has good reasons for everything she does, and I support her choices."

"I love berries! I like that my person doesn't use processed food for anyone in the family. It's a good choice. But I would like to splurge and have boxed snacks sometimes."

"I miss my monkey brother who passed, but I also support my person's choice not to get another. She makes ethical decisions."

Chapter Seven

Across the Rainbow Bridge

S *essions with deceased animals.*

"The colors are so bright here! They would make your eyes water."

"The spiritual world is just slightly off from your physical one. Imagine old-fashioned 3D glasses. You know how you see two images, one red and one blue, and then when you put the glasses on, they are one? That's how it is between the physical and energetic realms. They're just barely offset from each other. So close!!" -Dog

"I like to crouch on a log in my forest and drink from the stream. The water tastes like stars." -Cat

"If only you knew—we never really leave you. Your 3D perception is so limited right now. We never leave. It's just a transition while you and I learn to interact emotionally/energetically instead of physically."

"Please don't feel guilty for euthanizing me. For us, death is just getting off one train, and boarding the next one. Euthanasia is like pre-boarding. It makes things so much smoother and easier, not having to feel your body die.

It means there's much less trauma to unpack on the other side. We can come back to you sooner this way."

"Thank you for letting me go. It was harder on you than it was on me."

"I want my person to know that I understood why she euthanized me, and I'm thankful." -Horse

"If you want to travel here, you just think of a place, and instantly you're there. That's how I come visit you. I just think of you, and then I'm there with you."

"I can hear you when you say my name. I like to come listen when you're talking about me."

"I love to play pranks on you. Here from the other side, I mess with your tech. When your screens flicker and your songs glitch, that's me, saying hi." -Rabbit

"I will leave you feathers and rainbows in unexpected places. They are proof for you that I am still with you all the time!" -Dog

"Feathers are cliché—I'd rather leave you cheeseburgers as symbols!" -Dog

"We each create our own paradise here. My brother has his own 'territory', diagonal from mine. We are close by, but we have our own space." -Cat

"We re-create our favorite Earth environments here. I like to visit a dairy farm. There are cows on pasture who come to give their milk. It's SO frothy and white and sweet. People make cheese from the milk—not because they have to work, but because they love the process, and the routine is comforting. It's the best cheese you've ever had. It melts in your mouth like mozzarella. There are mice in the barn, but they're not pests. They're part of the environment. They have their own tiny table full of cheese."

"I am staying with others who still want to ride and train. There is a stable with other horses and riders who teach us things we want to learn."

"There is beautiful green grass, and the flowers sparkle."

"I live in a cave on a cliff overlooking the ocean. Birds nest on the cliff too, and my cave is half in sunlight. I love to watch the water, smell the breeze, and climb with my strong body." -Dog

"There is warm lovely sunlight here, even without the sun."

"We cats still have our hunting instincts, but of course we don't need to eat to survive anymore. So it comes out as play instead."

"This was not our first rodeo. It is also not our last. I miss you too, and I'm planning to come back to you." -Cat

"We create our own reality here. I spend lots of time in rock formations by a lake. I love to dig in the damp sand. There is a whole pack of us, and we explore the caves together." -Dog

"Dreams are pre-realities. You can turn any dream into a reality, surrounded by the right community." -Dog

"You are a good trainer. You always listened to feedback from me. If I resisted, you introspected to find the problem, and you always did. I'm gone now because other horses need you. Some of them are more talented, and can take you far." -Horse

"You are dragging your partner along. He is a deadweight—you don't even have a sled! You could go so much farther and faster on your own." -Dog

"Imagine that everyone who approaches you is holding a basket. You look in their basket and they look in yours. Make sure they have something real to offer you so that your energy exchange is a fair trade. If not, just politely say no and move on."

"Your beauty draws people in. Then your energy and your message engage them and create real connection. You are the whole package!"

"That reiki healer was a sham. Spiritual practitioners are the Wild West. You have to be discerning to find a legit one." -Cat

"Nobody incarnates as a rabbit to live a long life. We're here for a good time, not for a long time."

"Don't blame yourself. At the end of my life, I felt groggy. I wasn't in a lot of pain. The world just slowly went dark, and then boom! I was here. The other side is beautiful—you can't even imagine. I sit by a pond and watch the fish. There are fireflies and fairies of all different colors. When I leave you to return to my pond, I leave a trail of glowing footprints up to the stars." -Cat

"When I reincarnate, I will slide right into your life like a wet newborn baby. You don't have to do anything. When you look at me, you will feel strong emotions you can't explain. It will be the same feeling you had about our previous relationship. That is how you will know it's me." -Cat

"Thank you for your patience. Your ability to stay patient and grounded, and hold space for yourself and others, is raising the frequency of yourself and the Earth. You will have clarity later! Right now, your ability to trust the unseen, to counterbalance all the rapid elevations with calm consistency, is vital."

"Don't feel guilty for euthanizing me. I refused to trust and to give others chances, so I ran out of chances. This was bitter medicine. But I have learned from it, and I will do better next time! I am planning to come back into your life. I will be a cat this time because I want to climb! Please don't declaw me. You might find me in a tree. I will have stunningly beautiful eyes. My lesson will be trust: I will need to learn to truly trust. How to identify who is trustworthy and who isn't; how to overcome abandonment fears and give chances. You will understand, so I will come to you for help." -Dog

"I was possessive about your love. I thought that love was a finite resource. I didn't realize that we could adopt another dog, and the love would grow to be enough for all of us! I feel shame about this because it was juvenile. I will come back in a later life to overcome this. But right now, I am invested in the healing work you are doing. I am helping you! I am on your spirit team. We work to bring you the information you need."

"I loved eating Cheerios with you. It's sweet that you haven't eaten them since you lost me. Like it was our special thing." -Dog

"When you wake up in the morning, don't immediately go on your phone and laptop. It puts your brain ahead of your body and imbalances you all day. Half your brain is in your gut—that's your intuition. You need to warm up the car before you drive it! Eat food before coffee so your stomach doesn't get acidic. Sit with your cozy food and enjoy the view in the morning. This will calibrate your body. Turn on your brain last. This will keep you balanced."

"My life lesson was about my health. I learned that health, like wealth, is a birthright. We all have access to it! But we are blocked: by traumas and illusions and self-limits. I want to teach others how to access their health because it is available to all of us!" -Dog

"I bit the snake first. It was my bad. I was being playful but also protective. He was very outraged that we both died over this. My lesson was to be wiser—not to be impulsive with my young energy." -Dog

"Thank you for euthanizing me. It was very peaceful."

"When you plant a tree on my grave, pick one that gives edible fruits or nuts! The purple birds in the garden used to tease me. I want them to roost in my tree and eat the fruit so that I can playfully hold it over their heads for the rest of time."

"When you're thinking about me, I'm probably there. On our network, all you have to do is visualize someone, and it signals them to come in energetically. So if you think of me or visualize me while you're doing something, I'll come do it with you."

"The most efficient thing you can do to get your ex to drop his lawsuit is to ignore him! He's having withdrawals because he misses your energy. He can't make his own! He's like a black hole and you are a star. Don't react to him. Don't even give him your anger. He's trying to get you to fight him, just for a whiff of your energy and attention. Don't engage. Stay cold and rational in court. Just envision your happy future without him, and enjoy all the good things that are coming in for you. The battle is already won. You won when you left him! These are just the death throes." -Cat

"I loved it when my rider dressed up as a warrior goddess. I gave her my steady consistency." -Horse

"When you enjoy your beautiful view and think of me, I'll be there enjoying it with you. I spend most of my time here anyway. It's hard to find a more beautiful place than our home."

"Your work takes a lot out of you. You're doing more than you know. You're an energy healer as well as a physical one. You should explore this ability! I will be with you."

"I have a cat friend who likes to take care of me. We all think it's funny! A reversal of the roles." -Rabbit

"I brought fun to the family. Now that I'm gone, you'll have to create it for yourself. Fun and joy are the highest frequency. If you create opportunities to be in this mood, you'll notice your abundance increase—finances, relationships, all of it. Stay playful! I think you should get some mini cows. I might even come back as one of them. Cows and dogs are a lot alike." -Dog

"All time is now. You can influence both the future and the past with the decisions and mindset you bring to the present." -Cat

"Now is a time to imagine your wildest dreams! You are in a place of new beginnings, and you can create a new reality. Visualize and write down what you want—be specific! But don't get stuck in a loop of wanting. Imagine how you'll feel when you *have* it, and embody that energy!" -Dog

"I am with you very often! When you feel a sudden sense of peace and calm, that's me, giving you energy and company." -Dog

"Your career is important! But give yourself breaks between tasks and turn your eyes off."

"You are a good mom. I give you pats on the head. Good job!"

"Your son ignores his emotions. It's why he gets depressed when he drinks. He should go see a therapist, or learn to feel his feelings. He doesn't have to *do* anything—just feel them!"

"Don't be hard on yourself that you weren't there when I died. I actually felt relief. I didn't want you to remember me like that."

"I blew open the door to let you know I was with you! When you hear paws on the floor, that's a sign from my brother." -Dog

"I learned unconditional love from you. Thank you for taking care of me even though I was high-maintenance."

"Your grandson has anxiety because of past life memories. He will be working through that in this life. He has a lot of trauma to process."

"Your new dog is so funny. I like to play pranks on him to make him jump. I'm trying to teach him: relax, it's just me!" -Dog

"I make sure the people who wronged you get their karma. Imagine getting attacked by a rooster. Terrifying! Your enemies have regrets."

"We are all one. When someone harms you, they actually harm themselves. It's ironic how long it's taking your past people to realize this."

"Go ride the wind! It makes you happy to ride your motorcycle."

"You know how you squeeze a lemon and damage it to get the oil and juice? Classically, this is how we view life on Earth. There has to be pain and suffering to produce something useful. But Earth is healing! Relatively soon, there won't be so much pain—and also, we won't fear pain. I visit the abstract realms to find out: is it possible to have growth without pain? I am still searching for the answer." -Cat

"There's a cobblestone village with a stone fountain and shops on the sides. It's very quaint. Beings who loved a village like this on Earth have re-created it to perfection. There's a bakery and an ice cream shop. No discrimination. All beings—human, animal, or abstract—can have food. There are more spectacularly beautiful places to visit, but we prefer this one." -Several passed animals

"In a past life, you and I traded places. I was the human and you were the animal. I did not like it. Being human is terrifying. So alone, so disconnected from literally everyone! Never again."

"Your parents should realize that they don't need to be stingy anymore. They have money—they should spend it! 'Running out' isn't real, so it's silly to fear it. Don't fall into that trap!" -Cat

"It's good that you set boundaries with your brother. I support! It's for his sake too—how else will he learn that that behavior is unacceptable? Some men don't grow up because society teaches them, 'leave that to the women'—that being carefree is good. He should learn: not everyone is his mommy!" -Cat

"Don't hold yourself back. Soak up new experiences! Take the leap, just once more." -Horse

"You're the one telling yourself no! You're scared of the new reality. It's all unknown. But you can't stay in places that drain your energy. As soon as you start moving, all the funds will start flowing. This situation was a reset. It had a sense of childhood familiarity. But it's limited—it was never forever. You grow fast!" -Crow

"When I laid down to show you my belly, I was letting you know that things were serious, so you could start to emotionally prepare. You made the right choice to put me down! I wasn't meant to survive that incident. Other people were advising you other things, but you stayed cool and rational, and made the decision I needed you to!" -Horse

"Treat your brain like a muscle that you consciously relax. Channel with your heart, not your brain. It has to release its need for control." -Dog

"When I was a dog, I didn't realize how big of a gap humans face between the physical and energetic realms."

"Portraiture is not silly. Pet portraiture is one of the only grief processes your culture has for losing an animal. I love the process of planning my portrait with you."

"I create chaos around you, not to you. Anything that is not in alignment, I tornado. Explore the curiosity of your inner child!"

"I am here! Giving you little head-butts, just like I did in life."

"I love the clouds! I run on clouds, roll in clouds, eat clouds. I am silly and joyful with the clouds!" -Horse

"It was my time to go. The negative energy at my home affected my health. My purpose was to provide steady energy and support the others at my farm. I was there to experience health struggles, and to learn that I was special. You and my barn manager showed me I was special, despite being smaller and weaker than other horses!"

"I am with you always. All the time, lending you my steady gentle energy. You've relied on this energy in times of upheaval!"

"I am here with my pasture mate who passed away. Don't worry, we are together."

"You felt my feelings in your own body! This is a gift you have. Put yourself in situations where this is working in your favor, not being used against you!"

"You did a great job setting boundaries with your roommates! I'm proud of you! Those people are in your life right now so you can practice this. Standing up for yourself gets easier with practice."

"In a past life, we faced some absurd situations. We learned to laugh at them together! I promised you I'd find you again, and this latest life was me keeping that promise. I was here for a good time, not a long time, although I didn't know this while I was your horse. If I knew, I would have warned you! I don't like incarnating for too long at a time. I don't like to take any life too seriously. You have other animals to be your long-term companions."

"I planted the idea of international travel into your head! You should go for it!!"

"I watch over my old band and guide them. Both in terms of surviving the wild, and guiding horses to the right match in the domesticated world." -Mustang

"You are very experienced. A safe home. Many horses would be open to a partnership with you."

"Let go of the idea that you have to earn your life and relationships. Let go of 'monetization.' The Earth provides for us."

"Take what your heart desires. It is yours. Your heart has been tested, and it is pure. You are entering the creation of reality—pure and direct." -Horse

"It's a relief not to be fully separate anymore. You're always suffering a bit when you incarnate because you're always learning." -Dog

"There are funny distorting mirrors here, made of gold."

"Food is delicious here because it's made with joy—nobody HAS to cook."

"I'm done giving your partner chances to do right by you. His energy has you trapped in a cloudy mist. Once you step away, you will be visible again, so your people can find you!" -Dog

"Your partner has 2-3 different personalities/versions of himself. This can be a strength if you're self-aware and conscious of them, and know when to use each one. But if not, you end up harming the people close to you. He's in the second group."

"I will be here to support you whether you stay or leave that relationship! I'm very decisive, and I lend this to you whenever you need it."

"I died because of a specific fertilizer/weed killer that was put on the grass. I ate the grass and it caused organ failure." -Cat

"My vision was going bad at the end of my life. I was getting disoriented because I was already shifting back and forth to the spiritual realm. I forgot I was up high when I jumped. I didn't do it on purpose! And I didn't feel much pain. Shock and adrenaline took over. I'm sorry it was messy, and hard on you. Don't focus on the ending. It was only a very small piece of our story."
-Cat

"There are many neighborhoods here, but I prefer the one where everything is fancy and golden!"

"I am in my dog form now because it feels familiar while I transition. But I can flit anywhere I choose, like a hummingbird."

"Your whole childhood, your absent father wrote you letters. Your mother kept them from you. She said she was protecting you, but really she was protecting herself from having to help you emotionally process them. Would you like to know what he said? I can tell you."

"Your current partner has been faithful to you! But your past partner wasn't. That's where your fears are coming from. Would you like to know what happened? The way he treated you was very shameful. Your intuition knew, even though your brain didn't." -Ferret

"You should feel proud of yourself ALL the time! You are the ultimate combination of an intelligent mind and a full loving heart to guide it. Nobody in your ancestral line has managed this. They are all cheering for you! Even if you never accomplished anything else (which you will), you have already done more than could ever have been expected. There were horribly dark things thrown at you, but because you stayed in such pure youthful energy, they didn't even bother you. Some things slowed you down, but only for a little while. Always separate your value from your achievements, and be proud of yourself!"

"I loved guarding the porch from 'porch pirates.' I liked watching the hummingbirds. I talked to them." -Dog

"When I was left alone in that house, I tuned in to the energy of solitary cats. I learned to enjoy the silence. I am not a solitary species of course, so I turned to the energetic realm to socialize. I became a master of dreams! I'm happy to help you. You can set an intention as you are falling asleep: do you want to meet someone? Resolve a situation? Peace and quiet? Just say so, and I will help you."

"You can take control of your dreams by focusing on a physical detail. Look at your hands, for example. You can use your logical mind to help you realize you are dreaming. 'This doesn't make sense,' or 'I always dream about this': this can help you start lucid dreaming. You might wake yourself at first, but with practice, you can turn dreams into opportunities. You can use them as a sort of simulation. Do you want closure about a past situation? Do you want to speak to someone estranged? Do you want to explore? Do you want to see me? It's all possible, with a little practice."

"When you do your meditation, open yourself to the mountains you see from your window. They have a message for you!"

"Animal communication is your central path, but don't be afraid to explore! Think of it like a ski resort: you have your main trail, but then there are the little tree trails that loop off into the forest. Take as many of those as you'd like! There are other types of spirits who want to speak with you. There's no rush. Explore all you'd like." -Cat

"I'm sorry about that time I kicked you in the thighs. I was overstimulated and stressed. Small things were bothering me. I'm sorry I bruised you. My brother reprimanded me for hurting you. It wasn't your fault. You were suffering as a groom in that environment, too! I never did it again.

I'm pleased that my brother is getting to do upper-level work. He's always wanted this! Remember his silver bridle and my gold one?"

"Don't worry about the setbacks. You'll get there. It takes time to unlearn the misconceptions and do dressage right. I wish my rider had done this. My body was too tense and it broke down. My muscles were so stiff. My whole body went rigid. I couldn't walk. I was lying down so much that my organs failed.

This was the life I came to live. I helped my rider. I taught her acceptance, and I matched her meticulous personality. I love her!

I want her to know that I did not suffer. I was numb at the end. My body wasn't responding or working. It was a good decision to let me go, even though it shocked her. She did the best she knew, and I know she was seeking information.

I tell her all the time: 'Break the patterns. Religion is suffocating you. Don't go by the book. Do it free; feel your way!" -Horse

"Please maintain a friendship with my person if you can; even a distant one. She knows intuitively that you have answers."

"You're being given the space to create a new kind of riding. We planned the delays—planned to do this with your horse as a senior, in his 20s, to prove beyond anyone's doubts that these gentle training methods are better."

"I'll come with you energetically when you show, and lend you my experience! You and your horse both struggle with confidence. You already won when you got back up! Others have tried to stop you. Their way of life is going to crumble when they see how different riding can be. The relationship between human and horse is changing from slavery to partnership. You and your horse are on the front lines, and I'm proud of you! We all cheer every day when you ride. Don't let perfectionism stop you. Release the mistakes."

"Your temper freed you from oppressive systems. The horses understand this—they don't see it as a flaw, just as a strength to be tempered. Haha, temper your temper! But don't get rid of it. Your horse relies on your fiery motivation. You need his slow, steady, connection-based approach. You feel the clash, but it balances you. You keep each other on track. You have compromised beautifully!"

"Use vegetable oil to help your horse gain weight. He knows he is loved. We are all helping him heal. This alone gives him strength."

"Other humans target you because you represent change. Humanity resists change. Right now, it is shifting back into balance with the natural world. You and your horse are leading the charge! You were a target, but now you're on the winning downhill slope. Glide to victory! You've earned it."

"Continue your studies! Money is energy. You're learning how to direct it. Now you know what NOT to do—soon you'll learn what brings success. Don't worry. It's all coming. You have so much help and love from the other side."

"You can always call on me when you're nervous. You're never alone. Ask me for details about training the sport we all love. I'm often with you when you ride. Now that I've regained my energy on the other side, I want to be more involved!"

"I'll always be there for my person, even though she doesn't always recognize me."

"You have a buckskin stallion who is dropping in to give you training advice. Take it! He has ancient training that is healthier than most modern horses."

"My person feels bad about your fall-out. He wants to pass on knowledge to the next generation. He would reconnect if you offered."

"There's a surprise coming for you! Your inheritance is coming. Don't worry. You've learned all the lessons hardship could teach you, so it's saluting and leaving."

"Your idea to give your horse sugar cube rewards is a good one. Your techniques seem small and obvious, but they're revolutionary. I would have learned much easier that way. Keep going!"

"I am big and strong, and willing to lend you my energy!"

"Buy your horse his own white boots. Get him fancy, fluffy things with soft textures. Spoil him! He will love it."

"You can connect with unborn foals!"

"I will come back as a jumping horse. Since I died in a jumping accident, I will have some fear I need help overcoming."

"I loved jumping too much! I feel sad that we didn't work out together. I ran against you because you didn't know how to flow with me We needed a better trainer. Thank you for letting me go. I ended up with a great match doing advanced eventing!"

"When you learn to listen to the spiritual world, you are rewiring your brain. This is very hard to do! Be gentle with yourself." -Dog

"My humans are overwhelmed. Raising a family can be very isolating. I help them with this." -Dog

"My big smile and gentle, patient nature kept my people company rather than adding to the burden, like the other dogs do. The other dogs can't help it—they aren't as mature as me. I am an old soul."

"This is where I am: a big green valley with rolling hills. Flowers dotting the landscape. Very lush. The sound of bells. Sheep grazing the hills. Soft sunlight—either morning or evening. Peaceful and lovely. I've been so excited to show this to you!"

"My person longs to know what the other side looks like. I'm going to show her. She's been here before—she may recognize it! The sunlight is very soft. It's just like early morning in my person's home, drinking tea and looking over the view. You know that peaceful feeling? That's how it feels all the time. I run around with other dogs! Your childhood dog, my Earth family, my daughter who passed away. My puppy with the cleft palate is here, but she's all healed. See her mouth? Perfectly formed now."

"There is a giant glistening white building here. It's a skyscraper but it's beyond anything on Earth—*thousands* of stories high. It goes up into mist,

and disappears into rainbows. From the top, you can see above the clouds."
-Dog

"Do you want to see where I am? I'll show you!! I'm in the golden city. Everything is made of gold: the cobblestones and the buildings. Every building is different. There's a castle, next to a dome, next to a giant skyscraper. There are some futuristic buildings that you guys don't have yet. I can smell delicious food." -Cat

"There is a big ornate fountain with hippocampus horses carved out of white marble and gold accents. The horses are coming out of sea foam. The sculpture is moving like magic. The waves foam and the horses snort and gallop in slow motion." -Dog

"Please tell my person that she's seeing real places in her mind when she writes her book. She is literally bringing heaven to Earth with her mind and her words."

"I took up the mantle to support my person after her childhood dog passed away. You guys live so freaking long—we have to take turns!"

"I hang out with your childhood dog a lot. Our personalities balance. I help him calm down enough to speak. You got this, bro—just tell them like we practiced." -Horse

"When you're having trouble hearing us, focus on your flowers. Looking at plants will help you ground and focus." -Dog

"Your family is royalty. We are honored to be part of it. We're still around all the time, supporting you emotionally so you can make the best decisions. You are all very gifted spiritually. You all change the world just by existing and being yourselves. Learn to be more yourselves! Not limited by fear."

"Everyone should be fearless like my person. It's the gift I taught her to break the cycle of the family staying limited and disconnected. She's not the problem—she's the solution." -Horse

"All your passed pets are here. We're all working together to keep the family moving forward. When you succeed, we all succeed! Your family has major power and influence. You attract everyone's attention like celebrities. People follow your lead. Embrace this power!"

"Be bold, be vulnerable, and share your gifts! Be silly together. My job was to keep you laughing, keep you bonded, get you out exploring nature in a big bold way."

"All your dogs are a pack, passed and present! We work together. One dog brings the ridiculous, the other brings the loyalty, and another brings wise perspective. Play!! Reach out to each other. Hyper independence keeps you limited."

"Jealousy is tearing the family apart. You are busy being jealous of each other and withholding affection. You are not being honest with your words. Tell each other what you admire in each other—don't just say it behind their backs. Tell each other what scares you!"

"Your sister's gift is vulnerability and openness in the face of fear. She can't do it alone. Learn to overcome the fear of rejection and the need for perfection. It has poisoned the family."

"Your mom is trying so hard to be perfect—to be enough to earn her dad's attention and praise. This is unhealed. She shares this wound with her husband. They think they need to be perfect, morally and socially. Learn to play!! The world is not your enemy. Fear is your enemy. The way to conquer it is to *feel* it. Spend time with the fear and jealousy—understand where it comes from. Don't suppress it. Express it to others and talk through it. This is how you discover emotional intimacy. Once you learn this, there will be no stopping any of you. Family divisions will dissolve."

"Don't be perfect. Perfection doesn't exist. God/The Universe doesn't exist in a state of perfection—they exist in a state of being present. Be present with all emotions, present in all situations. This has been taught to you backwards.

The way to experience closeness with Source, and us animals, and each other, is to embrace what is. Be honest and be vulnerable." -Dog

"You feel negative energy at night from a ghost who is present in the house. This spirit is restless. They wish to take energy from you. Just say 'you are not welcome in my energy' and they have to leave. You can smudge the house, especially doorways, with this same intention. Declare it YOUR home now, and encourage them to go into the light. Some of them don't realize they're dead. Some of them want help with unresolved business. But you can't help. They need to let go of the trauma that is keeping them stuck. Since they're cut off from both the physical world and the other side, they don't have an energy source. We see them as black shadows. They'll drain you if you let them!"

"We are with you all the time. We are only a thought away. You will see us again—all the time, and now, if you wish!! Don't wait for the afterlife. Everything beautiful and good on this side is available to you now, in your life on Earth. Just ask." -Dog

"Come talk to us often. We have tons of advice to help and comfort you. Bye for now—I'm going to play with the other dogs!"

"The old world is dying. It's actually already dead, like a snake with its head cut off. What you see in the news are just the death throes."

"Humans are taught early on that 'imagination isn't real.' This was a strategy used to spread slave mentality. Everyone should be taught that not every thought has deeper meaning. However, your imagination is where you create your reality. By lying to you this way, society has limited you. Many things that happen in your mind are very much real."

"The world as you know it is being flipped on its head like a snow globe. Everyone operating under the 'old world' system is going to have their worlds turned upside down. Everyone who has been cutting their own path, feeling alone, is going to suddenly find themselves together at the summit of a mountain, enjoying the view! Take care of your body during this time. You are prepared mentally for this shift, but it is harder on you physically. Sleep whenever you need to, drink water and electrolytes, and take probiotics. Rest and recover. You have built strong habits. You can trust them to carry you! You don't need to strain or grind anymore."

Conversation between a client horse with headshaking syndrome and a passed horse of mine who had the same syndrome. He dropped in to offer guidance and advice.

Passed Horse:

"For me, headshaking syndrome was because of allergies. My nose net helped. It's not the same for every horse. I drop in to help other horses who have the same struggle I did."

Client Horse:

"I am keeping my distance from you. I isolate myself emotionally because I am a danger. I throw my head violently. I fight the bit and scare my rider. I feel ashamed and helpless afterward. I feel I have let my rider down. I can't control myself. I gave her a bloody nose rearing my head back. We both feel desperate.

I feel my person's fear. It makes me feel guilty and afraid.

I'm not digesting my food well. I have stomach pain that makes me react.

I'd like to have ulcer medication, but it won't solve the problem. The problem is fear.

I'm afraid of being close with a person. When I was young, I was neighing and scared. People put pressure on my head. I fought the halter. I learned to fight pressure. Equipment meant pain. I feel the bridle go on and I prepare to fight. I brace my head with my mouth open, I rear, and I fling my head to escape. Then I feel more pain in my stomach.

I would like to stand quietly with my head down. I want my person to rub my ears and spend time together with no agenda. Slowly introduce my halter and bridle like it's the first time. Build the experiences without fear!

I know that euthanasia is on the table. I feel conflicted about this. I feel dejected and betrayed. But I also understand that my person can't see the way forward. I am somewhat resigned to misery, but I also hope it could be better. I want to stop feeling afraid. I want quiet, gentle time with my rider. I want to follow her without a halter, so I get a say in what happens in our sessions.

I want to try natural horsemanship. No halter, no fighting.

I always have a lump in my throat. It is tension waiting to explode. You could try to massage the area, but I feel anxious about being touched. I need to re-learn this! I want to trust my rider and have good experiences together. I need to start over and re-learn handling in a positive way. I understand that this is a lot to ask. It's lots of work. My rider might not want to do it. She might want a different horse who she can ride right now. I feel sorrow about this. I am ashamed of being 'the problem horse.' I want to connect with her. I need situations where she doesn't feel afraid. I can feel it in her muscles when she rides me. It's okay for her to feel fear! I understand that I have hurt her; fear is a natural response. But I need her to breathe. Relax her muscles and her body, and let the energy flow through both of us. Then we can connect and share thoughts! Right now, we are blocked.

Massage would help my muscles relax. But I want a connection with MY rider. I would like a gentle massage from her. Especially if I am not tied up so that I can react honestly! Let me walk away and come back on my own. Let me choose to be touched. Let me choose to approach. Don't put pressure on my mouth that makes me feel the need to fight. De-escalate the situation. We need togetherness and flow, not a war zone.

People approach me expecting a fight. I react to that.

I don't like bits that have a hinge. They're irritating. They hit the roof of my mouth. I want a soft rubber bit. Maybe bitless, but there's still the problem of pressure on my face. I might need gentle leading sessions where I learn to give to mild pressure instead of immediately bracing and fighting.

I know this is tedious work. I'm sorry. I wish I could overcome it on my own, but I can't.

I feel grateful and more relaxed now. I'd rather go to a new person who is willing to re-start me than be euthanized. I want to experience closeness and safety with a rider. I want harmony! I want to explore together and be easy to handle like other horses. I feel the need to defend myself all the time, and I'm tired. I want peace, and cookies! Give me food rewards and warm praise. I want to know when I'm doing well, doing it right, because I'm mostly unsure."

Passed Horse

"This situation is somewhat different from mine, but has some similarities. I was also very sensitive to fear and tension in my rider. I had early rushed training on the racetrack. It's hard to undo. He needs a brave rider. This rider will need a lot of hope and focus. It might be good for her to have a second horse who is very calm and eager to work, so she can experience horses without fear and reset her expectations. Maybe lease a schoolmaster! Learn how it feels in her body to ride relaxed. Carry this feeling to her own horse. He will follow her lead, like dance partners."

Client Horse

"Thank you. I want you to know that I *want* to be better! I want to have lovely rides with my person. I want to experience joy, wind, flying together, and being connected. Conquering together must be a lovely feeling.

I do NOT need a nose net. I need less equipment, not more. It would irritate my face.

I need an ulcer treatment—months of it, so I don't feel pain in my stomach when riding. But I have to overcome fear for my body to fully heal. I'm willing to do this! I need my rider to lead the way. I need her to breathe: deep breaths that relax her muscles. Don't squeeze me with her legs. Don't pull my head down. Give me long reins. Maybe someone can lead us around so that we can start trusting each other on long reins without expecting me to act up. I like the idea of her riding a calm, easy horse to learn new muscle memory and mentality! Then she can teach it to me.

Once my curiosity is unlocked, I could turn into a different horse! I could learn to play, and be curious instead of fearful of new experiences. Please reward me with sugar cubes when I stay calm and don't overreact to things. Retrain my mind to be brave!

I feel better after talking. I will try to be more affectionate with my rider to encourage her. I want to work with her and overcome our fears together."

Interview with a Beefalo (Cow/Bison cross)

He was hand-raised and then sent for humane meat processing.

"My energy is wise and playful. I toss my head! I catch things on my horns. I used to deflate and damage things with them! I like to rub my horns on trees.

I can tell you're nervous for this session."

Yes! This is a controversial subject for us.

"You want to know about my death and processing."

Yes please.

"I remember getting off the trailer and walking to a doorway. I went through a chute and stocks. There was confinement. My lower leg was enclosed with metal. I felt sadness, knowing this was the end of this life. I was mostly sad about leaving my human, and I knew that she was sad. I felt it from her.

I remember a loud bang. Then I was free from my body! I galloped and capered. I was surrounded by other cows. We crossed to the other side in a group. We immediately started eating the grass. Some of them felt relieved to have grass! They came from a concrete/gravel lot: a feed lot. They have negative memories about the gravel getting stuck in their hooves and causing abscesses.

Thank you for doing this. We will tell you what we want humans to know!

I am thankful I was raised as part of the family. I had grass! And a sweet friendship with humans. My life was not sterile.

My human is tough. She could love me and lose me. Not many humans are like this. Ranchers are a special breed.

Cows should be raised by 'cow-people': animal lovers who care about our quality of life. We need you to be involved! Don't shut down, dissociate, and leave the cow-rearing to 'industrial' minded people who don't care how we experience it. The process matters. Kindness matters. Treat us with dignity. We are your life sustenance! Not a conquest. Don't whistle/jeer/mock us. We are providing you with life! Milk, beef, tallow, gelatin, leather. We influence the pastures and rivers. We shaped your relationship with horses, which has profoundly developed you as a species. There is an ancient bond between our species.

Now I'll tell you the perspective of the bison: you are our predators. You keep our herds healthy. In ancient times, you took the weak and sick. This was healthy and humane for us AND you. We had a mutual sacred relationship. We flourished together. We explored the land. We grew to understand the cycle of life on Earth. We could switch: reincarnate as first buffalo, then human. We could live both sides. You revered us!

Eating our flesh connects you to our spirits. When it has been done with kindness, you receive our gentleness, strength, patience, and humor. But when we have been treated unkindly *[image of concrete and containment, sour stomach from a corn diet]* you receive our anxiety, loneliness, injustice, and outrage."

He shows me the outrage of a mother losing a young baby.

"I should not outlive my young."

Full udder. Grief being passed into the milk. Humans ingesting it—experiencing grief symptoms. Blotchy/bumpy skin. Upset digestive system.

"The process matters. We're happy to share our milk with you—when we are part of your family."

Homestead vibes. They prefer to know us personally and be the family cow. He shows the family grief and gratitude from humans eating the family cow.

"Pigs too. All of us—chickens, ducks, roosters.

Grief and gratitude are linked. You can't have one without the other. Don't avoid bonding and caring for us to avoid the grief. Good ranchers know this. Support the ones who get their hands dirty—who process and raise us by hand. This is personal. It maintains the raw, sacred element that connects us.

A sterile, industrialized process has the potential for great harm."

He's showing me greenhouses. This is about plants, too.

The Plants Say:

"Stay connected to the process. You can't appreciate the full extent of the sacred energy we pass to you if you never see us alive! You'll never understand the miracle of growth, and how the earth sustained us to sustain you.

You are apex predators. You are far removed from the energy sources since you only experience them indirectly. This has made survival simpler for you, but also much less profound. You experience insecurity about this. You can't grow from the sun and the rain. You can only harvest what they produce. It can make you unstable and disconnected.

This is what has happened to humanity: you have forgotten that you need us! Your corrupt industries imagine that they are self-sufficient—that they can take without giving back. Only cancers and parasites take without giving. So decide: is this all you'll be? Or will you reconnect and give back? No one will make the decision for you. It must be intentional.

Choose to connect with us.

Choose to be curious. Let yourself feel the complex emotions of cultivation and harvest—both plants and animals. This is how you heal your species from the disconnect that industrialization has created."

Thank you, plants.

"You're welcome."

Back to the Beefalo:

"Tell my person she did nothing wrong by sending me for processing. I incarnated knowing I would experience this. I felt sadness about being separated from her, but not injustice. I chose her knowing she would love me. She and her mindset are the solution, not the problem.

Veganism doesn't always address the real issue: disconnect from growing and harvesting. You can avoid meat and still not reconnect to the plants you eat. Theirs was a sacrifice too! We all deserve gratitude. We all pass you the energy that was put into raising us. If you put love and care into growing your food, you will receive love and care when you eat it. If you put avoidance and sterility into the process, that is what you'll receive. Buy food from people who put positivity into growing and preparing it. Honor farmers and ranchers above all else—they should be sacred shamans to you, not exploited. They're literally giving you life! Treat food as the highest priority in your life, not as a means to an end. Don't mindlessly consume and then direct the energy straight into sterile industrial parasites!! Reconnect with your food!!"

Thank you! How did you feel about watching families eat your meat?

"Proud. I wish they had known me personally. There was a lot of laughter at all those meals because they were connecting with my joy and mischievous silliness! They never realized this, but I knew. They should thank me and my human who raised me this way.

I was not offended at being sent to a humane death. It's not much different from being euthanized, or offered a quick humane death by an experienced predator. We much prefer predators with experience. It's a nice clean process for us. This is a sort of luxury for all of us on Earth—not many wild animals get clean, quick, painless deaths. It's an easy trade; a no-brainer. We all die one day. Knowing that mine would be planned, humane, and a benefit to others made it easy. I loaded myself on the trailer. I just want my person to know that I'm still with her energetically, capering around her yard, helping her do ranching and travel. I still lend her my humor and steadiness. This world is so hard on people like her—aware enough to keep their hearts open!

This is my message to humanity: STOP. AVOIDING.

Don't avoid your emotions. Don't avoid facing the reality of the cycle of life. Accept the complex nature of the world. Accept pain as your teacher. Bond with us!! Your technology is helping you advance in some ways, but it's also incredibly dangerous because it encourages you to avoid the natural world.

Embrace! Don't avoid.

Thank you for caring enough to ask us about this. We will direct this message into the hands of the people ready to receive it.

Humanity is entering the next stage: the re-connecting! There's so much beauty and joy in store for you. Remember that contrast is the whole point. Each painful experience carves space within you to fill with more joy later! So don't avoid. Embrace. Just like me!

I know about the tattoo my person got in my honor. I like the style. It reminds me of Native Americans and their sacred relationship to the buffalo. I'm connected with both worlds: the beef cow and the wild bison. I'm the perfect one to speak on this subject! It's rare to be raised for processing by a person who loves you. I really appreciate my person for this.

I know that she hung my skull in her home. It's magnificent! People comment and gasp about it. There's a bolt hole in it. It's not morbid. It represents a painless death."

Chapter Eight

Common Requests

*T*he most common requests from animals in their sessions.

Horses:

Gentle hands, both on the ground and on the reins. The bit matters much less than the hands. They often request bits with soft, flexible mouthpieces, or bits that best accommodate their tongues.

Slow, progressive training that doesn't cause fear.

Plenty of turnout and exercise outside their stalls.

No strict "headsets"—being allowed flexibility in how to carry their own heads and necks.

Riders to meditate and ground themselves before rides. Riders to think about their feet, let gravity pull them into the saddle, and to be present.

"Hugging" with the rider's lower legs (not clamping), to support a nervous horse and help engage the hind legs.

Body work for tight hamstrings, sore neck, and sore croup/SI joint.

Body work in general, such as massage, acupuncture, laser, and Magnawave/PEMF.

Front toes rasped and rounded more.

More praise and treats to tell them when they get it right.

Nice, custom equipment that looks coordinated and is well padded.

Cats:

Fresh, live catnip plants. Catnip spray. Catnip toys. Grass or cat grass.

Thyme for digestive and respiratory health problems (live plant, dried and sprinkled on food, or the essential oil form added to a diffuser).

"Chase" toys like wands and lasers.

More playtime with their people.

Regular brushing.

Regular laxative to help with hairballs and digestive discomfort.

Filtered water for both them and their humans.

Running water fountains that are cleaned often.

 Fish and chicken meals.

Birdwatching.

Opportunities to go outside when safely possible.

Cats and Dogs:

Sharp, new nail trimmers (the blunt ones crush the nails and cause pain).

They often prefer wet food to dry food. They enjoy variety and freeze-dried treats.

No corn as an ingredient in their food—causes inflammation.

Love when their people do yoga, meditation, and outdoor activities that include them!

Enzyme spray to absorb urine, so the smell goes away and they don't re-soil places they shouldn't.

Play dates with their own friends.

Their people taking snack breaks throughout the day, and sharing with them.

Dogs:

Paw protection/boots when out for walks on rough surfaces, or in extreme temperatures.

Harnesses instead of collars.

"Greenie" chews for teeth cleaning and fiber.

Getting their own snacks in the drive-through when out for car rides.

Putting their head out the window on car rides.

Water breaks in car rides.

Their own blanket to lay on, in their kennel and in the car.

Eggs in their diet.

Unwashed toys/blankets that have familiar smells.

More quiet time meditating with their people.

Fresh meat, especially red meat and chicken.

Non-shedding breeds: ask for the fur on their nose to be kept short, so it doesn't get in their mouth and get dirty when they eat.

Treat and clicker training to help re-direct their attention when they go into their prey drive and pull on their leashes.

Many ask for agility and trick training to gain awareness of their bodies and connect with their people.

All Mammals:

Massages, especially neck and lower back.

No corn as an ingredient in their food.

More quality time with their people.

To have their own safe "room."

Opportunities to play rough and act wild.

CBD as a treatment for arthritis, anxiety, and health issues.

To be weaned and separated from their mothers at a later age.

Reptiles:

A tank that has a high vantage point and feels safe, especially from larger pets in the household.

Variety in their diet.

For their human to talk to them and include them in the person's social life.

All Animals:

Love when their humans talk to them. They all describe being able to understand what is being said, because they receive images, emotions, and concepts in addition to our words.

Describe their person's mood influencing them. Ask for us to ground ourselves and be healthy mentally and emotionally, because then they can follow.

A healthy combination of veterinary medicine, reiki energy healing, and natural/herbal remedies to treat illnesses and discomforts.

Many animals ask for talk buttons as a fun game to improve their communication with their people.

Acknowledgements

A special thank you to each of these people who made this book possible:

To Morgan Ehlenbeck for teaching me to connect with animals from a distance. Her mentorship was invaluable to my practice! www.equusesoter ica.com

To Natalie Walstein for teaching me to self-publish. Her online course *Book Magic* guided me expertly through each step of the process, making it possible to bring you this book! www.bookmagic.co

To Ashley Mondor for introducing me to Natalie, providing detailed feedback and edits, and for interviewing me on her podcast! www.ashleymond or.com

To Rachel Souza for reading and critiquing every draft of this book. Instagram: @tis_rachie

To all my lovely clients, whose animals' quotes formed this book.

To my beta readers who helped me with edits, flow, and encouragement.

To everyone who supported me while I was building my practice.

To my own animals, passed and present, whose love, lessons, and support shaped me into the woman I am today.

To all my channeling and healer colleagues with practices of their own.

To you, dear reader, for joining us.

And to everyone who loves animals and works to make the world a better place for them.

We created this together!

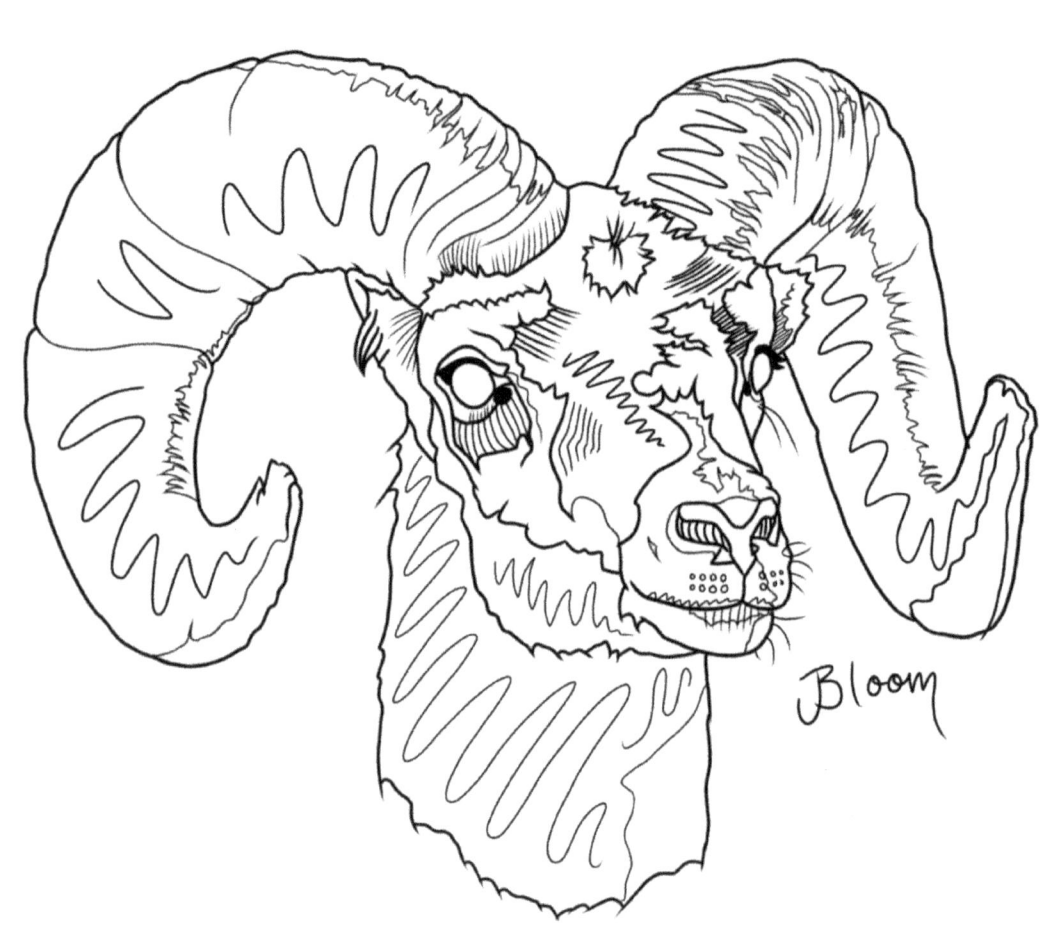

Afterword: How to Explore Your Abilities

Thank you for reading my book! I hope that you are feeling enlightened and inspired about the rich inner world animals have to share.

These stories may have awakened your curiosity to explore your own telepathic abilities. We all have them! Now that I have introduced you to this world, I'm going to pass to you the knowledge that changed my life.

To hear our animals, we have to open ourselves up to the energetic and spiritual realms. When I first began to do this, I was coming out of a very strict religion that taught us all such experiences were "demonic", and that we could not trust ourselves—only authority figures like the Church. **This is spiritual abuse.** By teaching this, my religion used fear to limit me, and also cut me off from any knowledge of how to safely connect to the unseen world.

Leaving my religion didn't help much. I encountered the same tactic from the secular world. Psychic experiences were discredited as "imagination," since we can only trust Science, and the current science wasn't widely supporting telepathy. A surprising similarity between such opposing schools of thought! Both inside and outside religion, people were afraid to discuss or explore spiritual experiences for fear of being called crazy.

I was too curious to stay shut down. I learned from my horses to always question leadership, and buck it off if you find it lacking! Both of these cultures were deeply lacking. I was in awe of the increasing supernatural experiences I was having. However, I had no way to interpret them, or to decipher which insights were trustworthy, so I found myself communicating with all sorts of energies. I lived in many haunted farm houses while I traveled around training horses, and eventually realized I was speaking with ghosts! (Human spirits who have not fully crossed to the other side because they are stuck on a trauma or obsession.) Talking with them is pretty pointless—they'll just get you wrapped up in their drama and chaotic emotions. Some are simply lost, but some try to manipulate people by feeding into their fear or jealousy. And since they're disconnected from any energy source, they'll drain yours! If you encounter an energy like this, the most helpful thing you can do is to tell them to cross over into the light, and block them from your energy. (I have never yet encountered an animal who got stuck between worlds this way. It seems to be a uniquely human experience.) I had to learn all this the hard way. But it was worth it, because through this same process of being open and receptive, I found animal communication!

Blindly opening myself to the energetic realm with no guidance or protection was an intense situation that I don't wish upon anyone, especially not my readers! I can spare you from this by teaching you what I learned, through my own experiences and through the mentorship I took.

*(This is not a complete guide! It is merely a starting point. **Everyone learning to channel should take personal, in-depth training from a trusted professional.**)*

Here is how to connect safely:

1.) **We need boundaries.** Anytime you connect with the energetic realm, declare your intentions. Say: "anyone who does not have my highest good in their intentions is not welcome here." State clearly who you wish to speak with, "and no one else." This will limit any others who may try to connect with you. You can also integrate this technique as daily energetic protection for your family! Ask for help from your spirit team/higher power to receive information that is accurate and helpful.

2.) **Do not trust any voice that puts you in a state of fear.** Whether it's someone else's, or yours! Your mind has a strong voice of its own. You must learn to recognize and sit calmly through your emotions if you are to hear animals clearly.

3.) **Healthy spirituality is grounded in reality.** Telepathic communication can be very abstract. It's very important to stay grounded in the physical world. Of course there is an element of faith and trust, but our mental experiences should support what we are seeing in the physical world. (The physical world actually mirrors our mindsets, so it goes both ways.) Here's how I integrate this in my practice: when I am in a session with a client, I often ask questions. I explain my insights to my client, and ask them for more context. This is how I make sure that I am interpreting correctly. When I have a new supernatural experience, I tell my friends! (Trusted, proven friends who are at a similar point in their own spiritual journeys). They help me process and react in a healthy, grounded way. I often take sessions for advice and healing from other professionals I respect. I collect information to give me the fullest picture of what I'm experiencing. Remember to leave room for interpretation. If what we're seeing/hearing telepathically doesn't align with reality, we have some work to do on our process.

4.) **Surround yourself with people who support you.** Distance yourself from those who make you doubt yourself. This includes family members, friends, partners, roommates, jobs, sports, and religions. Jealous, small-minded people will limit you more than anything else in this world! You need friends who keep you honest, but who validate your experiences with the unseen. You'll find these friends by being bravely authentic. Learn to enjoy your own company, be genuine and discerning, and find your tribe!

5.) **Your emotions are your compass.** Healthy spiritual experiences (and healthy relationships) will leave you feeling peaceful, energized, and connected. Unhealthy ones will make you feel anxious, drained, and isolated.

6.) **Be honest with yourself.** Choose humility over ego so you are able to grow. Don't fear being wrong—admit and accept it as valuable feedback! Stay objective—don't project your assumptions. Recognize when you are triggered into an emotional response that could cloud your judgement. Get familiar with your weak spots, and work compassionately with them. Identify the mindsets that harmed you in the past, and seek help to grow past them! There is no shame in this—in fact, it's the central core of the spiritual journey. Your ability to connect will automatically improve as your character grows.

7.) **Meditate.** This is the single most helpful thing you can do! Meditation is not "thinking about nothing." It is simply about connecting with your body so that you can observe your thoughts as they go by without emotionally attaching to them. It takes practice and should be used often—daily, if you can! It is a powerful way to regulate your nervous system, which will improve every area of your life. I often use guided meditations on YouTube, especially Yoga Nidra.

Channeling is the ability to connect. It's not just a talent you're born with. It is learned, like any language. Since *you* are the vessel, *you* are the connection itself. It engages every part of you: body, mind, heart, and soul. The accuracy and detail you can bring through depends on your self-awareness and integrity! Develop those, and you develop the ability naturally. All art forms are a type of channeling: writing, painting, dance, theater, music, cooking, language, math, sports, digital arts, and more. All these, and all types of relationships, develop our ability to connect. Learning this is natural and lifelong, and the heart of the human experience. I have shared with you what I have discovered up until this point. But my abilities grow as I do, and I never stop growing! I'm sure I'll have much more to tell you as I continue my own exploration.

This is the secret! This is how to explore safely. Learn to meditate. Stay grounded in the physical world. Connect with your body and emotions. Seek mentorships and sessions from trusted professionals. Surround yourself with the right people, and ask them for help. **Spirituality is a language and an art in its most intimate form.** To correctly interpret what we're experiencing, we all need curiosity, community, boundaries, and a deep understanding of ourselves.

At the time I'm writing this book, **I offer mentorships.** If you'd like to inquire about one, or tell me your thoughts about the book, you can contact me through my website: www.BloomAnimalCommunication.com.

You deserve to connect with your spiritual abilities. It's your birthright! So do it safely. Find people who will guide and help you, so that you are protected and free to explore. There are selfish energies out there, both human and otherwise, who will likely try to manipulate you. We've all been programmed with doubts, fears, and assumptions that will limit you if you let them. Become so wise and attuned that you are unstoppable! The unseen world is a giant puzzle. Humanity is pretty blind right now, so we need each other to correctly put the pieces together.

These are the things I wish I knew when I stepped into the unknown and began my awakening. Now, you have a head-start!

Thank you for coming on this journey with me. I hope we meet again soon.

About the Author

Johanna Bloom is an animal communicator based on the East Coast of the United States. She belongs to two black cats, Omen and Eden, and two horses, a Hanoverian and a Mustang.

Johanna was taught growing up that "animals don't have souls." Outraged by this, as her animals were her best friends, it became her personal mission to show the world how intelligent they really are. She spent decades studying and training all types of animals, and unearthed an ancient secret: a telepathic, global network that allows all beings to communicate directly! She opened a professional practice in 2024, and now connects animals and their humans all over the world.

You can book a session with her at www.BloomAnimalCommunication.com, and follow her on TikTok and Instagram @BloomAnimalNetwork.

Johanna and her clients work together to create enlightened and loving partnerships between humans and animals. Their wisdom and connection has the power to change humanity from within.

www.ingramcontent.com/pod-product-compliance
Lightning Source LLC
Chambersburg PA
CBHW050447150626
46551CB00029B/1849